ORACLE® DBA AUTOMATION

QUICK REFERENCE

Prentice Hall

ORACLE DBA SQL QUICK REFERENCE SERIES

Oracle DBA SQL Quick Reference

Russel ▪ Cordingley

Oracle DBA Backup and Recovery
Quick Reference

Russel ▪ Cordingley

Oracle DBA Automation
Quick Reference

Russel ▪ Cordingley

ORACLE DBA AUTOMATION QUICK REFERENCE

RUSSEL ■ CORDINGLEY

PRENTICE HALL PTR

Prentice Hall

Professional Technical Reference
Upper Saddle River NJ 07458
www.phptr.com

Library of Congress Cataloging-in-Publication Data is available.

Russel, Charlie.
  Oracle DBA automation quick reference / Charlie Russel, Robert Cordingley.
    p. cm. -- (Prentice Hall Oracle DBA SQL quick reference series)
  Includes index.
  ISBN 0-13-140301-X (pbk.)
  1. Relational databases. 2. Oracle (Computer file). I. Cordingley, Robert. II. Title. III. Series

QA76.9.D3R865 2004   2004043673
005.75'6--dc22

Editorial/Production Supervision: *Patti Guerrieri*   Acquisitions Editor: *Jeffrey Pepper*
Interior Design: *Gail Cocker-Bogusz*   Editorial Assistant: *Linda Ramagnano*
Cover Design Director: *Jerry Votta*   Manufacturing Manager: *Alexis R. Heydt-Long*
Cover Design: *Nina Scuderi*   Marketing Manager: *Dan DePasquale*
Technical Reviewers: *Lorraine Juzwick, Kevin Owens, Thomas Hatzigeorgiou, Bert Scalzo*

Prentice Hall PTR offers excellent discounts on this book when ordered in quantity for bulk purchases or special sales. For more information, please contact: U.S. Corporate and Government Sales, 1-800-382-3419, corpsales@pearsontechgroup.com. For sales outside of the U.S., please contact: International Sales, 1-317-581-3793, international@pearsontechgroup.com.

All company and product names mentioned herein are the trademarks or registered trademarks of their respective owners.

Printed in the United States of America

First Printing

ISBN   0-13-140301-X

Pearson Education Ltd.   Pearson Education Canada, Ltd.
Pearson Education Australia Pty. Limited   Pearson Educación de Mexico, S.A. de C.V.
Pearson Education Singapore, Pte. Ltd.   Pearson Education — Japan
Pearson Education North Asia Ltd.   Pearson Education Malaysia, Pte. Ltd.

Charlie would like to dedicate this book to Robert, Ross, Quin, Prashant, Mahesh, Maggie, Opal, Donna, Jen, Luisa, and Harold.

Contents

Chapter 4

Day-to-Day Administration   **151**

Introduction

The Oracle database is a complex and ever-changing product that has grown increasingly complex and powerful over the years. In the bad old days, the working Oracle database administrator (DBA) had a limited set of tools to automate the day-to-day tasks of maintaining the health and integrity of Oracle databases. Thankfully, that has changed over time, and now with Oracle 9i, and especially Oracle 10^g, nearly everything associated with the database can be automated. Unfortunately, Oracle has provided little documentation on exactly how best to accomplish this. We hope this book will help you on your road to discovering the many ways that Oracle can be automated.

WHY AUTOMATE?

Very few DBAs are allowed the luxury of managing a single database, or even two, or three. In these days of increasing workloads, many of us are managing 20, 30, or more databases, and they're frequently scattered all over the world. With the number of databases in use on the rise, it's important to streamline every step of the process as much as possible. Automation improves your productivity in two very important ways: It reduces the time you need to spend waiting for the database to do something, and it improves the overall quality and repeatability of what you do.

IMPROVED PRODUCTIVITY

The first advantage to automation is improving the overall productivity of the Oracle DBA. When the DBA performs a task manually, there is, inevitably, a substantial amount of time spent waiting for the database to do its thing. There's also a good deal of time usually spent by the database waiting on you to tell it what to do next. In both cases, time is wasted and the overall productivity of the DBA is seriously affected. Besides, let's face it, the stuff you can automate is usually the boring stuff you don't really want to be doing anyway! So let Oracle do the work for you.

IMPROVED QUALITY

The hidden benefit to automation is a significant improvement in the quality of the DBA's work. An automated task is a predictable and repeatable task. When you do a task manually, *especially* one you do repeatedly, you will eventually make mistakes. Sometimes they're small mistakes, sometimes big ones. But if you automate the task, it will always be performed the same way, time after time after time.

USE WHAT'S ALREADY THERE

Right from the very beginning, with the initial software installation, Oracle allows you to reduce or eliminate the need for a DBA to watch and wait. Once Oracle has been installed, you can configure the network and create one or more databases automatically, with no human intervention.

After the software is installed and the database created, the DBA finally reaches the real meat of the job. For the experienced DBA, there's a very real tendency to keep using the tools he or she has always used, even if the tools were originally created for use with Oracle 7. The fledgling DBA can run into similar problems, since it's difficult to discover all the different automation opportunities included with Oracle while simultaneously dealing with demands from users, developers, and management.

In spite of these challenges, or even because of them, it's vitally important to automate as much as is possible. It's equally important to avoid recreating a capability that's already available. The two most recent versions of Oracle have added an almost unbelievable wealth of options for the overworked DBA to automate his or her way to a quieter pager.

TEST EVERYTHING FIRST

With the multitude of new capabilities in recent versions, there's a temptation to implement everything that the documentation says will help improve operations or performance. Resist the temptation—at least long enough to allow time for testing of each and every new feature prior to implementation. Some of the new features will help in all situations, some will help in all but a few situations, and a few might create problems in certain circumstances. Testing prior to implementation is essential.

WHAT'S IN THIS BOOK?

Chapter 1 will introduce the Oracle Universal Installer (OUI), and explain the use and creation of *response files*, which are files that provide your responses to the installer. Response files allow a highly automated installation session to proceed with little or no user intervention. You can even use these files as templates for manual installs, when you need to deviate slightly from the response file's intended course.

In Chapter 2, Oracle Network Configuration Assistant (NetCA) will receive similar treatment. While not as automation-friendly as the OUI, NetCA does have a reasonable amount of flexibility, using response files similar to those used by OUI.

Chapter 3 is all about the Oracle Database Configuration Assistant (DBCA). The DBCA is one of the most versatile parts of a DBA's toolkit, and extremely easy to automate. You can use DBCA-specific response files, but the real strength of the tool lies in its unique use of template files. The DBCA can create databases, clone them, and even "reverse-engineer" an existing database into a template, or even a set of scripts.

Finally, Chapter 4 can be regarded as a "survey course" of Oracle features that can be used to automate some of the tasks that consume a DBA's time day in and day out.

TALK TO US

We have made every attempt in this short volume to provide as complete a reference as we could, always with the goal of keeping it brief and easy to find the information you need. Our goal was to give the working Oracle DBA a tool to make him or her more productive, and we sincerely hope you find it useful. Every effort has been made to be both complete and accurate. If you do find an error or omission, or have a comment on the book, we very much want to hear from you. Please write us at: *OracleAutomation@scribes.com*. We don't promise to answer every question or comment, but we do read them and very much appreciate them.

ACKNOWLEDGEMENTS

This book is not the work of one or two people, but an entire team, many of whom we as authors never get to meet in person, but to whom we are indebted. First, we'd like to thank our agent for this book, Neil J. Salkind, of Studio B. It's due to his persistence and advocacy that this book came about.

From Prentice Hall, a truly exceptional team did an amazing job on this book, going way beyond the norm. Jeffrey Pepper was his ever-persistent and patient self. Jeff, we told you we'd make the deadline! Patti Guerrieri was our editor again, and we couldn't have been happier. Linda Ramagnano works with Jeff and keeps everything happening quietly behind the scenes, where we barely notice. And for that, we are eternally grateful! There are others at Prentice Hall whose names we'll never know, and we're sorry about that. They are critical to the success of this project and we are no less indebted to them for not knowing them personally. You're a great team and we really appreciate all you do.

Our reviewers, Bert Scalzo and Lorraine Juzwick, did an excellent job, making good suggestions and giving us greater confidence as we worked on beta software to make sure we covered all the new features in Oracle 10^g. If we missed anything, it's not their fault. Sheila Cepero, our Oracle Publishers Program beta contact, provided timely assistance and access as we struggled to meet our deadlines. Thank you, Sheila, it has really been a pleasure.

Over the years, we have been honored to work with some truly outstanding Oracle DBAs, especially Quin Bligh, Maggie Verdier, Mahesh Chenga Reddy, Prashant Dangash, and Ross Woody. Each had a positive impact on this book and beyond. We truly appreciate their professional abilities and their friendship.

And finally, Charlie's wife, Sharon Crawford, who provided support, assistance, advice, and most importantly, love, throughout this book. Without her, it would not have happened.

Chapter One

Oracle Universal Installer

One of the beauties of the Oracle database is that nearly everything associated with it can be automated. Oracle installation is one of the easiest tasks to handle with little or no human intervention. Sadly, Oracle Corporation has historically provided little documentation on exactly how to accomplish this.

This chapter will discuss the main steps in automating an Oracle installation. Some platforms may require specific preparation before the installer can run. This preparation is usually straightforward and simple, but consult the installation guide for your specific platform *before* proceeding.

AUTOMATED INSTALLATION

When performing an automated install, you must provide the installer with a text file containing all the necessary instructions. Oracle calls these *Oracle Universal Installer (OUI) response files.* A response file is a plain text file, which must follow Oracle's syntax exactly.

To use a response file during an installation on Windows or UNIX, use the following commands (where "custom.rsp" is the name you've given your response file):

Windows	`setup.exe [-silent] -responseFile C:\OraInst\custom.rsp`
UNIX	`./runInstaller [-silent] -responseFile /u01/OraInst/custom.rsp`

The `-silent` qualifier is optional. When a silent install is indicated, the installer will not open any graphical user interface (GUI) windows under any circumstances. All needed information must be provided in the response file for a silent install. If any information is missing, the installer will exit, returning an error and the name of the log file to examine for details.

If the -silent qualifier is omitted, the installer will open normally and wait for the user to move through the install steps manually. Each page will be filled in with answers from the response file, but the installation will not proceed automatically. This is very useful if you want an installation "template" rather than a fully automated install.

In addition to the Oracle-provided sample response files, the installer can record a session to create a response file for use in later installations. To record a session, use the -record and -destinationFile qualifiers. For Windows and UNIX, for example:

Windows	setup.exe -record -destinationFile C:\OraInst\rec.rsp
UNIX	./runInstaller -record -destinationFile /u01/OraInst/rec.rsp

The installer will start and run normally. Choices made during the installation session will be recorded to the designated response file. After all selections have been made, a summary page will be presented. At this point, you can continue with the install or click the Cancel button to end it. Even if the installation is cancelled, the recorded response file is created.

REFERENCE

Command Line Parameters

The OUI supports the command line parameters described in Table 1-1:

Table 1-1   Installation Command Line Parameters

Parameter	Purpose	Additional Comments
-silent	Instructs the installer to run a silent install.	When this parameter is specified, the -responseFile parameter must also be provided.
-reponseFile <filename>	Tells the installer which response file to use.	The response filename should be fully qualified.
-nowelcome	Disables the installer's opening splash screen.	Redundant when used with the -silent qualifier.

Table 1-1 Installation Command Line Parameters (continued)

Parameter	Purpose	Additional Comments
`-record`	Tells the installer to record a new response file during the session.	When this parameter is specified, you must also use the `-destinationFile` parameter.
`-destinationFile`	Tells the installer where to write a recorded install session.	Useful only with the `-record` parameter.
`session_variable_name=<value>`	Sets a session variable.	Overrides the value set in the response file, if any.
`<component_name>_<component_version>_<variable_name>=<value>`	Sets a component-specific variable.	Overrides the value set in the response file, if any.

Response Files

Oracle ships with sample response files. These response files are different for Oracle 9i and Oracle 10^g. Table 1-2 lists the sample response files for Oracle 10^g, and Table 1-3 lists the sample response files for Oracle 9i:

Table 1-2 Oracle 10^g Sample Response Files

Oracle 10^g Response File	Purpose
oracle.client.Administrator.rsp clientadmin.rsp	Installs client-only version of Oracle, including all administrative tools.
oracle.client.Custom.rsp clientcustom.rsp	Custom file for client-only installs. Must be edited extensively before use.
oracle.client.Runtime.rsp runtime.rsp	Runtime-only installation of Oracle client. Generally used only for "embedded" installations.
oracle.server.Custom.rsp custom.rsp	Custom file for server installs. Must be edited extensively before use.
oracle.server.EE.rsp enterprise.rsp	Full Enterprise Edition (EE) installation. Needs minor edits before use.

Table 1-2 Oracle 10^g Sample Response Files (continued)

Oracle 10^g Response File	Purpose
oracle.server.PE.rsp	Full Personal Edition (PE) installation. Needs minor edits before use.
oracle.server.SE.rsp	Full Standard Edition (SE) installation. Needs minor edits before use.
dbca.rsp	Runs the Database Creation Assistant (DBCA) to create a database non-interactively. Requires an associated database template, and needs extensive editing before use.
netca.rsp	Runs the Network Configuration Assistant non-interactively. Needs minor edits before use.

Table 1-3 Oracle 9i Sample Response Files

Oracle 9i Response File	Purpose
clientadmin.rsp	Installs client-only version of Oracle, including all administrative tools.
clientcustom.rsp	Custom file for client-only installs. Must be edited extensively before use.
clientruntime.rsp	Runtime-only installation of Oracle client. Generally used only for "embedded" installations.

Table 1-3 Oracle 9i Sample Response Files (continued)

Oracle 9i Response File	Purpose
custom.rsp	Custom file for server installs. Must be edited extensively before use.
enterprise.rsp	Full enterprise edition installation. Needs minor edits before use.
standard.rsp	Full standard edition installation. Needs minor edits before use.
dbca.rsp	Runs the Database Creation Assistant to create a database non-interactively. Requires an associated database template, and needs extensive editing before use.
netca.rsp	Runs the Network Configuration Assistant (NetCA) non-interactively. Needs minor edits before use.
emca.rsp	Runs the Enterprise Manager Configuration Assistant non-interactively. Needs minor edits before use.
omicustom.rsp	Runs the Oracle Management and Integration Configuration Assistant non-interactively. Needs minor edits before use.
oid.rsp	Runs the Oracle Internet Directory Configuration Assistant non-interactively. Needs minor edits before use.

Syntax

OUI response files are plain text files. Installer settings are specified as name/value pairs, in the following form:

```
<name> = [ <recommended>  : ] <value>
```

<name> is always a single string, with no spaces, and is case-insensitive.

The <recommended> portion is a literal, which if present, must be either DEFAULT or FORCED followed by a colon. If DEFAULT is specified, the value will be presented as a changeable default during a non-silent installation. A FORCED value may not be changed by the user. If unspecified, the DEFAULT setting is assumed.

<value> can be a number, Boolean, string, or string list. The different value types are represented as shown in Table 1-4:

Table 1-4 Value Types Supported by OUI Response Files

Type	Example
Number	99
Boolean	TRUE

Table 1-4 Value Types Supported by OUI Response Files (continued)

Type	Example
String	"Sample string"
String List	{ "string1", "string2" }

Note that Boolean values are completely case-insensitive.

In Oracle 9i, the response file is organized in sections, similar to old-style Windows ".ini" files. Each section has a specific set of allowable keywords and values. The sections are shown in Table 1-5:

Table 1-5 Oracle 9i Response File Sections

Section Name	Purpose
General	Contains the version number of the response file.
Include	Allows you to include other response files with the current one.
Session	Lists values specific to the various dialogs of the OUI.
Components	Lists component-specific variables.

For Oracle 10^g, the section concept has been eliminated entirely. Name/value pairs, which would have appeared in the general and session sections of an Oracle 9i response file, can now appear anywhere in the response file, in any order. At the time of this writing, there does not appear to be any way to include other files within an Oracle 10^g response file. Items that would have appeared in an older version's components section now have the component name appended to the beginning, with a colon separating the component name and the rest of the name/value construct. For example:

```
oracle.networking.netca:OPTIONAL_CONFIG_TOOLS={"netca"}
```

The same setting in Oracle 9i would look like:

```
[oracle.networking.netca_9.2.0.1.0]
OPTIONAL_CONFIG_TOOLS={"netca"}
```

A response file can also contain comments. A comment is any line that begins with the # character. The supported syntax for OUI response files, by section, is shown in Table 1-6:

Table 1-6 Supported Syntax, by Section

Name	Value Type	Description
[General] Section		
RESPONSEFILE_VERSION	String	Response file version number. As of this writing, the correct value for 10^g is 2.2.1.0.0, and the correct value for $9i$ is 1.7.0.
[Include] Section		
FILEn	String	An arbitrary number of files can be included by appending a unique number to the end of each FILE directive and specifying a fully qualified filename as its value.
[Session] Section		
FROM_LOCATION	String	Indicates the source from which the product(s) will be installed. The string provided should be the fully qualified filename of the products.jar file on Disk 1 of the installation.

Table 1-6 Supported Syntax, by Section *(continued)*

Name	Value Type	Description
FROM_LOCATION_CD_LABEL	String	When installing directly from CD in a multi-CD session, this value indicates the label for which the installer should look when the CD is changed.
LOCATION_FOR_DISK2 LOCATION_FOR_DISK3	String	If installing from disk, or if all CDs are mounted concurrently, these variables tell the installer where to find the second, third, etc. disks. If not specified, the installer will automatically attempt to find successive disks in "../Disk*n*," relative to FROM_LOCATION.
NEXT_SESSION	Boolean	Instructs the installer to offer (non-silent) or attempt (silent) another install session immediately after the current one.
NEXT_SESSION_ON_FAIL	Boolean	If the current install fails for any reason, the installer will not attempt or allow another install if this value is set to FALSE.

Table 1-6   Supported Syntax, by Section (continued)

Name	Value Type	Description
NEXT_SESSION_RESPONSE	String	Fully qualified filename of another response file. If NEXT_SESSION and/or NEXT_SESSION_ON_FAIL are TRUE, the installer will automatically move to this response file when the current one is complete.
ORACLE_HOME	String	Location to which the software should be installed.
ORACLE_HOME_NAME	String	This variable is only important on Windows at the current time. It gives a name that identifies the ORACLE_HOME named above. If the home location already exists, then both the designated home directory and name must match.
APPL_TOP	String	If installing Oracle applications, this designates the installation home directory.
APPL_TOP_NAME	String	Analogous to ORACLE_HOME_NAME, this value names the APPL_TOP directory.

Table 1-6 Supported Syntax, by Section (continued)

Name	Value Type	Description
SHOW_COMPONENT_LOCATIONS SHOW_CUSTOM_TREE_PAGE SHOW_END_SESSION_PAGE SHOW_EXIT_CONFIRMATION SHOW_INSTALL_PROGRESS_PAGE SHOW_OPTIONAL_CONFIG_TOOL_PAGE SHOW_REQUIRED_CONFIG_TOOL_PAGE SHOW_ROOTSH_CONFIRMATION SHOW_SPLASH_SCREEN SHOW_SUMMARY_PAGE SHOW_WELCOME_PAGE SHOW_RELEASE_NOTES SHOW_DEINSTALL_CONFIRMATION SHOW_DEINSTALL_PROGRESS SHOW_CONFIG_TOOL_PAGE (10^g) SHOW_CUSTOM_TREE_PAGE (10^g)	Boolean	Tells the installer if it should display the indicated page during an interactive (non-silent) installation.
TOPLEVEL_COMPONENT	String List	This is a required variable that specifies the name and version of the main component to be installed.

Table 1-6 Supported Syntax, by Section (continued)

Name	Value Type	Description
UNIX_GROUP_NAME	String	UNIX group name to be used for the inventory directory. Used during a first-time install only.
DEINSTALL_LIST	String List	Contains names and versions of any components to be uninstalled prior to new software installation.
[*component*] Section		
DEPENDENCY_LIST	String List	A list of names and versions of other components on which the current component depends.
PROD_HOME	String	Location to which the current component should be installed. Most components must be installed inside ORACLE_HOME.
OPTIONAL_CONFIG_TOOLS	String List	Specifies a list of optional configuration tools to be launched by the installer.
INSTALL_TYPE	String	This variable must be present for the top level component(s) whenever there is more than one install type available.

Table 1-6 Supported Syntax, by Section (continued)

Name	Value Type	Description
COMPONENT_LANGUAGES	String List	When more than one language set is available, this variable indicates which language to install.
Component-specific variables	Varies	Many individual components have specific variables that can (or must) be set in the response file.

A complete list of component-specific variables is not provided here since they change, sometimes radically, with each release of the OUI. An exhaustive list can be found in the install directories. On Disk 1, in the stage directory, there are a number of ".jar" files. At the very least, there should be an install1.jar, but there may be more (install2.jar, etc.) files.

To look inside the jar files, you'll need to have a Java development kit (JDK) installed. Any JDK version should work, but Java runtime environments (JRE), will usually not include the jar command. Once you have a JDK, you can use the following command to extract the files:

```
jar xvf <jar filename>
```

The above command will extract everything from the jar file, creating a hierarchy of files in the current directory. Once that's done, you can explore the directories to find the "identifiers.xml" files. Every component that has some sort of settable variable will have one of these files. You can tell what component each one is for by the directory in which it is stored. Inside the file, you'll see, toward the end of the file, lines somewhat like the ones below:

```
<VAR NAME="s_dlgEMEmailAddress" DESC_ID="s_dlgEMEmailAddress_DESC"
TYPE="String" EXP="T" SEC="F" CLONE="T" CALC="T" VALDN="T" GEN_RES="T">

  <ASSOC_DEP NAME="oracle.sysman.agent" VERSION="4.1.0.0.0"
PLATS="{453,173,467,295,87,610,198,918,162,2,111,90,168,888,913,30,46,211,197,
110,912,615,50}" ASSOC="EMD_EMAIL_ADDRESS">

  </ASSOC_DEP>

  <ASSOC_DEP NAME="oracle.sysman.console.db" VERSION="10.1.0.1.0"
PLATS="{453,173,467,295,87,610,198,918,162,2,111,90,168,888,913,30,46,211,197,
110,912,208,615,50,601}" ASSOC="s_emailAddress">

  </ASSOC_DEP>

  </VAR>
```

This is a description of a single variable for the sysman.server component, since the file from which it was taken was in that directory. The variable's name is "s_dlgEMEmailAddress", it's a string variable, and a description of its purpose can be found by searching for "s_dlgEMEmailAddress_DESC" in the same file. If there is no description present, it is probably be a derived variable, not settable by the user.

Oraparam.ini

The oraparam.ini file contains initialization settings for the OUI. These settings will very rarely need to be changed from their defaults, but a description of all documented parameters is included in Table 1-7 for the sake of completeness:

Table 1-7 Oraparam.ini Supported Parameters

Parameter	Description
DISTRIBUTION	Set to TRUE if the oraparam.ini is on read-only media, such as a CD-ROM or the Web.
SOURCE	Path to the default products.jar file to be used for this installation. The path can be relative to the directory in which oraparams.ini is stored.
LICENSE_LOCATION	This parameter is not set by default. If used, it should point to a text file containing a license agreement to which the user must agree before proceeding with installation. When set, the license page will be presented after the initial welcome screen.
LICENSE_TITLE	Sets the title to be displayed when the license agreement, specified above, is presented.

Table 1-7 Oraparam.ini Supported Parameters (continued)

Parameter	Description
JRE_LOCATION	Path to the base directory of the JRE to be used for this install. This path can be relative to the directory in which the oraparam.ini is located.
OUI_LOCATION	Path to the OUI files.
JRE_MEMORY_OPTIONS	Memory settings parameter, passed to the JRE. This can be used to increase or decrease the amount of memory allocated to the installer.
DEFAULT_HOME_LOCATION	Default location for ORACLE_HOME.
DEFAULT_HOME_NAME	Default name for ORACLE_HOME.
NO_BROWSE	List of directories to which the installer will refuse to browse. This would generally be used to exclude extremely large directories or network-mounted directories.
NLS_ENABLED	If set to TRUE, national language support will be enabled in the OUI. If set to FALSE, the installer will display all prompts in English, even if the system's base language is set to something other than English.

Table 1-7 Oraparam.ini Supported Parameters (continued)

Parameter	Description
BOOTSTRAP	If set to TRUE, the installer will use a temporary directory to make a copy of itself and the JRE it needs before proceeding with the install. This will allow it to stop using the files on the installation media, thus allowing CDs to be changed. This variable must be set to TRUE for multi-CD installations. If the files are copied to a staging directory before installation, setting this variable to FALSE will slightly improve the speed of installation.
BOOTSTRAP_SIZE	This variable is used to indicate the size required for the bootstrap directory. Before installation begins, the OUI will check to make sure that at least this much space is available in the target staging directory.
OUI_VERSION	Sets the expected version of the OUI. This number must match exactly or the installer will exit.
USE_BUILD_NUMBER	If set to TRUE, the OUI will consider both the version number and build number when determining if it should overwrite an existing OUI installation.
APPLTOP_STAGE	When set to TRUE, the OUI will prompt the user to define an APPL_TOP directory.

SAMPLE FILES

Enterprise Database Installation with Starter Database

```
# This is an Oracle 10g response file.

# It does an "Enterprise" install of the server

# and creates a starter database, named orcl,

# using the general-purpose template.


# For 9i, this should be changed to 1.7.0.

RESPONSEFILE_VERSION=2.2.1.0.0


# On UNIX, this variable should be set to the inventory

# group, for an initial installation.

#UNIX_GROUP_NAME=<Value Unspecified>


# Must be a fully qualified path.

FROM_LOCATION=c:\OraInst\Disk1\stage\products.jar


# If installing from multiple CDs, set this to
```

```
# the expected volume label.
#FROM_LOCATION_CD_LABEL=<Value Unspecified>

# Must be fully qualified.
ORACLE_HOME=C:\oracle\ora10

# Only needed on Windows.
ORACLE_HOME_NAME=ora10

# Designates main component to install.
# The important part in this context
# is if it's oracle.client or oracle.server.
TOPLEVEL_COMPONENT={oracle.server,10.1.0.1.0}

# Can be set to:
#   oracle.server only
#     Enterprise Edition
#     Standard Edition
#     Personal Edition
#   oracle.client only
#     Administrator
```

```
#    Runtime
#    Either client or server
#    Custom
INSTALL_TYPE=Enterprise Edition

# These only matter if the -silent flag is omitted.
# If -silent will always be used, these can be deleted.
SHOW_SPLASH_SCREEN=true
SHOW_WELCOME_PAGE=true
SHOW_CUSTOM_TREE_PAGE=true
SHOW_COMPONENT_LOCATIONS_PAGE=false
SHOW_SUMMARY_PAGE=true
SHOW_INSTALL_PROGRESS_PAGE=true
SHOW_REQUIRED_CONFIG_TOOL_PAGE=true
SHOW_CONFIG_TOOL_PAGE=true
SHOW_RELEASE_NOTES=true
SHOW_ROOTSH_CONFIRMATION=true
SHOW_END_SESSION_PAGE=true
SHOW_EXIT_CONFIRMATION=true
SHOW_DEINSTALL_CONFIRMATION=true
SHOW_DEINSTALL_PROGRESS=true
```

```
# This only matters if the LICENSE_LOCATION variable
# has been set in oraparam.ini.
# In a -silent install, this must be set to TRUE
# if there's a LICENSE_LOCATION defined in oraparam.ini.
ACCEPT_LICENSE_AGREEMENT=false

# Response files can be "chained" by setting
# NEXT_SESSION to TRUE and specifying a
# response file with NEXT_SESSION_RESPONSE.
NEXT_SESSION=false
#NEXT_SESSION_RESPONSE=<Value Unspecified>

# Only set to TRUE if you want to continue,
# even if there's been an error in the first session.
NEXT_SESSION_ON_FAIL=true

# List of software that must be installed before
# installing the currently selected software.
DEINSTALL_LIST={oracle.server,10.1.0.1.0}
```

```
# Update this if you want multiple languages.
SELECTED_LANGUAGES={en}

# On UNIX, use this to designate the DBA group.
#sl_dbaOperGroups={}

# To migrate one or more databases, set this string
# list to the SID and ORACLE_HOME of each database to be
# migrated.
# Example:
# sl_migrateSIDDialogReturn={"orcl","C:\oracle\ora92"}
#sl_migrateSIDDialogReturn={}

# Where should the JDKs be installed?
JDK_HOME=C:\oracle\ora10\jdk

# HTTP listener port for the Microsoft Transaction Server
# recod service
s_recodHTTPPort=2030
```

```
################################
# Database Creation Variables #
################################

# Set both of these to TRUE to create a starter
# database.
oracle.server:b_createStarterDBReturn=true
oracle.assistants.dbca:b_createStarterDBReturn=true

# Designate what type of starter database to create.
# Oracle sample response files say that this is not
# to be set by the user, but no starter database
# will be installed if this is left blank.
# Can be set to:
#    General-Purpose
#    Data Warehouse
#    OLTP
s_cfgtyperet=General Purpose

# If this is set to D, then four separate admin passwords
# should be supplied in the superAdminPasswds varables.
```

```
# If set to S, then one password should be supplied in
# the superAdminSamePasswd variables.
s_superAdminPasswdType=D

sl_superAdminPasswds={"password1", "password2", "password3", "password4"}
sl_superAdminPasswdsAgain={"password1", "password2", "password3", "password4"}

#s_superAdminSamePasswd=<Value Unspecified>
#s_superAdminSamePasswdAgain=<Value Unspecified>

# Designate what type of disk storage to use.
# Can be set to:
#    File System
#    Raw Device
#    ASM
s_DataorASMret=File System

# To use raw devices, set this string to a raw device.
#s_rawDeviceName=<Value Unspecified>

#s_rawDeviceMapFileLocation=
```

```
# To use Automatic Storage Management, set
# this string list.
#sl_retdisklist={NO_VALUE,null}
#s_ASMString=

# If TRUE, example schemas will be loaded.
s_loadExampleSchemas=Y

# Define database SID and global name.
s_dbSid=orcl
s_globalDBName=orcl

# Designate database character set.
s_dbRetChar=Unicode standard UTF-8 AL32UTF8

# Mount point (directory) for datafiles.
# Files will be created in a subdirectory
# with the same name as the database SID.
s_mountPoint=C:\oracle\ora10
```

```
# Schedule automatic backups of the database?
s_dlgEMExtAutoBackupSelected=Y

# Allow the database to send email notifications?
s_dlgEMEmailNotificationSelected=Y

# Use a local or central Enterprise Manager (EM) console?
s_dlgEMOptionSelected=Local Management

# Name of central EM agent.
s_dlgEMCentralAgentSelected=No Agents Found

# SMTP server to use for email notification.
s_dlgEMSMTPServer=smtp-server.austin.rr.com

# Address to which email should be sent.
s_dlgEMEmailAddress=cord@badfiddler.com

# Local operating system (OS) account and password to
# use for backups.
s_dlgEMExtUsername=OSusername
```

```
s_dlgEMExtPassword=OSpassword


#########################
# Gateway Variables #
#########################

# Designate Sybase database and directory.
#s1_sybSerRetVal=<Value Unspecified>

#s_sybRetDir=<Value Unspecified>

# Designate MS SQL Server database.
#s1_sqlDBRetVal=<Value Unspecified>

# Designate Open Database Connectivity (ODBC) database.
#s_odbcInstLoc=<Value Unspecified>

#s_odbcDsn=<Value Unspecified>
```

Minimal Client Response File for Windows

```
RESPONSEFILE_VERSION=2.2.1.0.0
FROM_LOCATION=c:\OraInst\Disk1\stage\products.jar
ORACLE_HOME=C:\oracle\ora10
ORACLE_HOME_NAME=ora10
TOPLEVEL_COMPONENT={oracle.client,10.1.0.1.0}
NEXT_SESSION=false
NEXT_SESSION_ON_FAIL=false
DEINSTALL_LIST={oracle.client,10.1.0.1.0}
SELECTED_LANGUAGES={en}
INSTALL_TYPE=Runtime
```

Oraparam.ini

```
[oracle]

DISTRIBUTION=FALSE

SOURCE=../../stage/products.jar

LICENSE_LOCATION=

JRE_LOCATION=../../stage/Components/oracle.swd.jre/1.4.1.3.0a/1/DataFiles/
Expanded

JRE_MEMORY_OPTIONS=" -mx96m"

DEFAULT_HOME_LOCATION=\oracle\ora10

DEFAULT_HOME_NAME=Ora10

NO_BROWSE=/mnt

NLS_ENABLED=TRUE

BOOTSTRAP=FALSE

OUI_VERSION=2.3.0.7.0
```

Chapter TWO

Network Configuration

The manual creation of Oracle's various network configuration files can be somewhat daunting, especially to those inexperienced with Oracle. Oracle provides the Network Configuration Assistant, or NetCA, to help with this task. Interactive use of the assistant is reasonably well-documented and will not be covered here. NetCA doesn't lend itself quite so readily to automation as the Oracle Universal Installer (OUI), but it does have certain limited capabilities.

AUTOMATED NETWORK CONFIGURATION

To automate network configuration, NetCA uses a response file similar to the one used with the OUI. A NetCA response file is a plain text file.

Using a response file on UNIX is very simple, and very similar to how it's done with OUI. The command is:

```
10g   netca /silent /responseFile /fully/qualified/filename.rsp

9i    netca -silent -responseFile /fully/qualified/filename.rsp
```

Things are a bit more complicated on Windows, since running NetCA from the command line is apparently not fully supported. If, for example, your ORACLE_HOME directory is C:\oracle\ora10 and your JRE version is 1.4.1, then the NetCA command for both 10^8 and $9i$ is:

```
C:\oracle\ora10\jre\1.4.1\bin\java.exe -Duser.dir=C:\oracle\ora10\network\jlib -
classpath
";C:\oracle\ora10\jre\1.4.1\lib\rt.jar;C:\oracle\ora10\jlib\ldapjclnt10.jar;C:\or
acle\ora10\jlib\ewt3.jar;C:\oracle\ora10\jlib\ewtcompat-
3_3_15.jar;C:\oracle\ora10\network\jlib\NetCA.jar;C:\oracle\ora10\network\jlib\ne
tcam.jar;C:\oracle\ora10\jlib\netcfg.jar;C:\oracle\ora10\jlib\help3.jar;C:\oracle
\ora10\jlib\oracle_ice5.jar;C:\oracle\ora10\jlib\share.jar;C:\oracle\ora10\jlib\s
wingall-
1_1_1.jar;C:\oracle\ora10\jre\1.4.1\lib\i18n.jar;C:\oracle\ora10\jlib\srvmhas.jar
;C:\oracle\ora10\jlib\srvm.jar;C:\oracle\ora10\network\tools" oracle.net.ca.NetCA
/orahome C:\oracle\ora10 /responseFile C:\OraInst\netca.rsp /silent
```

It's a very messy command, and it's all on one line. If your ORACLE_HOME is somewhere else, or you're using a different version of the JRE, you can find the exact command in %ORACLE_HOME%\network\tools\netca.cl. The version in netca.cl will end with "oracle.net.ca.NetCA", and you'll have to add the rest of the above command to it to use a response file.

If the /silent qualifier is omitted, NetCA does not behave the same as the OUI. Unfortunately, omitting /silent seems to cause NetCA to hang indefinitely. Using a response file to pre-populate fields but allow running interactively just doesn't work. NetCA does not have the ability to record response files.

It appears that Oracle intends NetCA to be run automatically, mostly as a part of an initial installation. Using a custom NetCA response file during an OUI session is relatively simple. If you include the lines below, based on your database version, the OUI should automatically invoke NetCA using your chosen response file:

10^g
```
oracle.networking.netca:OPTIONAL_CONFIG_TOOLS={"netca"}
oracle.networking.netca:s_responseFileName="C:\OraInst\netca.rsp"
```

$9i$
```
[oracle.networking.netca_9.2.0.1.0]
OPTIONAL_CONFIG_TOOLS={"netca"}
s_responseFileName="C:\OraInst\netca.rsp"
```

COMMAND LINE PARAMETERS

The NetCA tool supports the command line parameters described in Table 2-1:

Table 2-1 NetCA Command Line Parameters

Parameter	Purpose	Additional Comments
/silent	Instructs NetCA to run a silent session.	When this parameter is specified, the /responseFile parameter must also be provided.
/reponseFile <filename>	Tells NetCA which response file to use.	The response filename should be fully qualified.
/orahome	Tells NetCA which ORACLE_HOME to use.	Must be specified on Windows, but is not needed on UNIX.
/orahnam	Tells NetCA the name of the ORACLE_HOME to use.	Not used on UNIX.

ORACLE'S SAMPLE RESPONSE FILES

Oracle ships with sample response files. Table 2-2 lists the sample response files:

Table 2-2 Sample NetCA Response Files

Response File	Purpose
netca.rsp	Fully commented NetCA response file, to be used as a basis for a custom version.
netca_clt.rsp	Not commented, and not intended to be edited, this file is for a typical client configuration. This file is only present in Oracle 10^g.
netca_typ.rsp	Not commented, and not intended to be edited, this file is for a typical server configuration. This file is only present in Oracle 10^g.

RESPONSE FILE SYNTAX

NetCA response files are plain text files. Installer settings are specified as name/value pairs in the following form:

```
<name> = <value>
```

`<name>` is always a single string, with no spaces, and is case-insensitive.

`<value>` can be a number, Boolean, string, or string list. The different value types are shown in Table 2-3:

Table 2-3   Value Types Supported by NetCA Response Files

Type	Example
Number	99
Boolean	TRUE
String	"Sample string"
String List	{ "string1", "string2" }

Boolean values are completely case-insensitive.

Under some circumstances, and for no apparent reason, some string values must be enclosed in doubled double quotes. The two variables that need this special treatment are noted in Table 2-5. For example:

`INSTALL_TYPE=""typical""`

In both Oracle 10^g and Oracle $9i$, the response file is organized in sections, similar to old-style Windows ".ini" files. Each section has specific set of allowable keywords and values. The sections are shown in Table 2-4:

Table 2-4 NetCA Response File Sections

Section Name	Purpose
General	Contains the version number and create type of the response file.
Components [oracle.net.ca]	Lists component-specific variables. The only component in evidence is [oracle.net.ca].

A response file can also contain comments. A comment is any line that begins with the #. The supported syntax for NetCA response files, by section, is shown in Table 2-5:

Table 2-5　Supported Syntax, by Section

Name	Value Type	Description
[General] Section		
RESPONSEFILE_VERSION	String	Response file version number. For NetCA, this should match the major version of the database being used. Oracle 9i Release 2 would use "9.2", for example.
CREATE_TYPE	String	Tells NetCA what type of response file to expect. Valid values are "TYPICAL" and "CUSTOM".
[oracle.net.ca] Section		
INSTALLED_COMPONENTS	String List	As the name implies, this is a list of installed components. Possible values are listed in the netca.rsp provided on the install media.
INSTALL_TYPE	String	Possible values are ""TYPICAL"" or ""CUSTOM"", and quotes must be doubled.

Table 2-5 Supported Syntax, by Section (continued)

Name	Value Type	Description
LISTENER_NUMBER	Number	Number of listeners to define.
LISTENER_NAMES	String List	List of listener names. These should be limited to LISTENER, LISTENER1, LISTENER2, etc. The number in this list should match the LISTENER_NUMBER variable.
LISTENER_PROTOCOLS	String List	For each listener, there should be one entry in this list. The entries are of the form <protocol>;<specific setting>. Possible combinations are listed in the netca.rsp supplied on the install media. Normally, only "TCP;1521" will be used.
LISTENER_START	String	The name of one listener to start. There appears to be no way to run NetCA silently, without having a listener started, so a value must be provided here. Quotes must be doubled on this variable.
NAMING_METHODS	String List	List of all valid naming methods for this ORACLE_HOME. Valid values are listed in the netca.rsp provided on the install media.

Table 2-5 Supported Syntax, by Section (continued)

Name	Value Type	Description
NOVELL_NAMECONTEXT	String	Novell Directory Services (NDS) name context. Quotes must be doubled for this variable.
SUN_METAMAP	String	Sun metamap name. Quotes must be doubled for this variable.
DCE_CELLNAME	String	Distributed Computing Environment (DCE) cell name. Quotes must be doubled for this variable.
NSN_NUMBER	Number	Number of net service names (NSNs) to configure.
NSN_NAMES	String List	List of NSNs. Typically, only "EXTPROC_CONNECTION_DATA" is set.
NSN_DBVERSION	String List	List of NSN database versions. Valid values are "80" and "81". "80" works with both $9i$ and 10^g.
NSN_SERVICE_OR_SID ($9i$) NSN_SERVICE (10^g)	String List	Service name (for $8i$, $9i$, and 10^g) or SID (8 and 7). Typical value is "PLSExtProc".
NSN_PROTOCOLS	String List	List of net services protocol parameters. Possible values are listed in the netca.rsp supplied on the install media. A typical value is "TCP;HOSTNAME;1521".

EXAMPLE NETCA RESPONSE FILE

```
# Custom NetCA response file, in which
# the listener's port number has been set
# to 1525, rather than the standard 1521.
[GENERAL]
RESPONSEFILE_VERSION="10.0"
CREATE_TYPE= "CUSTOM"
[oracle.net.ca]
INSTALLED_COMPONENTS={"server","net8","javavm"}
INSTALL_TYPE=""custom""
LISTENER_NUMBER=1
LISTENER_NAMES={"LISTENER"}
LISTENER_PROTOCOLS={"TCP;1525"}
LISTENER_START=""LISTENER""
NAMING_METHODS={"TNSNAMES","ONAMES","HOSTNAME"}
NSN_NUMBER=1
NSN_NAMES={"EXTPROC_CONNECTION_DATA"}
NSN_DBVERSION={"80"}
NSN_SERVICE = {"PLSExtProc"}
NSN_PROTOCOLS={"TCP;HOSTNAME;1525"}
```

Chapter Three

Database Creation

Even though it's not the most common task for a DBA, database creation is one of the easiest Oracle tasks to automate completely. You can use a Database Configuration Assistant (DBCA) response file, a DBCA template, DBCA-generated scripts, or manually generated scripts to create a new database. The process is relatively simple in Oracle 9i, and potentially even simpler in 10^g.

USING THE DBCA

The DBCA is a fairly simple and versatile tool for creating, copying, reconfiguring, and deleting databases. It's also very easy to automate most of these operations.

Creating a Database with the DBCA

When using the DBCA to create a database as part of an initial Oracle install, you must use a response file in conjunction with a database template. Response files can be used in other contexts, but aren't needed. The response file format is very similar to the formats of both the Oracle Universal Installer (OUI) and the Network Configuration Assistant (NetCA) files.

Using a response file is very simple, and very similar to how it's done with OUI. The basic UNIX command is:

```
dbca -silent -responseFile /fully/qualified/filename.rsp
```

The -silent parameter can be replaced with -progress_only, if desired. A silent install is similar to an OUI silent install in that it will open no GUI windows. Status and error messages will be printed to the console session from which the DBCA was started. Using -progress_only will allow the DBCA to open a single window that displays a graphical progress indicator. Regardless of the choice of silent vs. non-silent operation, the presence of a GUI is still required for the DBCA to run. This means that on UNIX, an XWindows environment must be present and accessible to the DBCA.

Using the DBCA without a response file is just as easy, but requires a much longer command line. A full reference is provided later in the chapter, but here is an example command line:

```
dbca -progress_only -createDatabase -templateName sampleTemplate.dbt -sid mydbsid
-gdbName mydbsid.mydomain.com -sysPassword mypass1 -systemPassword mypass2 -
emConfiguration LOCAL -dbsnmpPassword mypass3 -sysmanPassword mypass4 -
hostUserName myosuser -hostPassword mypass5 -backupSchedule 02:00 -smtpServer
mailhost.mydomain.com -emailAddress luckyrecipient@mydomain.com -
datafileDestination /db01/oradata/mysdbsid -recoveryAreaDestination /db02/
oradata/mydbsid/flash_recovery_area -characterSet AL32UTF8 -nationalCharacterSet
AL16UTF8 -storageType FS
```

This incredibly long command will create an Oracle 10^g database, based on sampleTemplate.dbt, which must be stored in the assistants/dbca/templates subdirectory of your Oracle home directory. The global database name will be mydbsid.mydomain.com, and the database's SID will be mydbsid. As the database is created, it will be configured to use a locally installed enterprise manager; non-default passwords will be set for the sys, system, dbsnmp, and sysman accounts; a default rman backup will be scheduled for 2 a.m.; and the database will automatically send email for various alerts to luckyreceipient@mydomain.com. By default, datafiles, control files, and redo logs will be created in /db01/oradata/mydbsid, and backups will go to /db02/oradata/mydbsid/flash_recovery_area. The database's default and national character sets will be con-figured as AL32UTF8 and AL16UTF8, respectively.

As exhaustive as the command line options are, there is still a lot of information left to be gleaned from the template file. In fact, most of the options specified in the example command can be left to default from the template. The only parts that can't be specified by the template are the template name (obviously) and the global database name. Since paths and filenames specified in the response file can use replaceable variables, overriding settings via the command line should not usually be necessary.

Generating Database Creation Scripts with the DBCA

In Oracle 10^g, the DBCA is capable of generating a complete set of database creation scripts based on an existing database template. In $9i$, the DBCA is not capable of generating such scripts from the command line. An Oracle 10^g example is:

```
dbca -generateScripts -templateName mytemplate.dbt
-gdbName mydbsid.mydomain.com -scriptDest /db01/script_dir
```

The above command will create shell scripts or command files, as appropriate to the operating system. It will also create structured query language (SQL) scripts, to be used with SQL Plus, and an init.ora file. When combined with the DBCA's ability to generate a template based on a live database, the script generation facility allows "reverse engineering" from a database to scripts.

Deleting a Database with the DBCA

Using Oracle $10g$'s DBCA to delete a database is a straightforward task. All parameters on the command line are required. In $9i$, the DBCA is not capable of deleting a database. An Oracle $10g$ example is:

```
dbca -deleteDatabase -sourceDB mydbsid -sysDBAUserName sys -sysDBAPassword
mysyspassword
```

Creating a Database Template Based on an Existing Database with the DBCA

The DBCA can be used to create a template file capable of recreating an existing database. Again, the command is very simple:

```
dbca -createTemplateFromDB -sourceDB myhostname:1521:mydbsid
-sysDBAUserName sys -sysDBAPassword mysyspassword -templateName mytemplate
-maintainFileLocations true
```

In this example, the DBCA will connect to the existing database, which must be open and available, then create a template named mytemplate. The parameter -maintainFileLocations tells the DBCA that it should not try to rearrange the database to be compliant with Oracle's optimal flexible architecture (OFA).

Creating a "Clone" Template Based on an Existing Database with the DBCA

As a logical extension of creating a simple template from an existing database, the DBCA can also create a template that includes a copy of the datafiles from an existing database. Unlike the previous command, which could be run against remote databases, creating a clone template must be done on the host where the database is running. The command is:

```
dbca -createCloneTemplate -sourceDB mydbsid -sysDBAUserName sys
-sysDBAPassword mysyspassword -templateName mytemplate
-maintainFileLocations true -datafileJarLocation /path/to/store/myjarfile
```

The -datafileJarLocation argument is purely optional. If omitted, the DBCA will store the datafiles in an archive in the same directory as the template, and with the same name. Only the file's extension is different.

AUTOMATING DATABASE CREATION WITHOUT THE DBCA

Creating an Oracle database without the DBCA may seem daunting at first glance, but it's actually a very simple process. At a very high level, the process consists of the following steps:

1. Create an initialization parameter file (init.ora).
2. Set up the environment.
   a) On UNIX, set the ORACLE_SID environment variable to the new SID.
   b) On Windows, use the ORADIM command to initialize a new database service.
3. Connect to the instance as sysdba.
4. Issue the create database command.
5. Create additional tablespaces, if any.
6. Run data dictionary scripts.
7. Run optional, additional dictionary scripts.

A Minimal init.ora

In Oracle 10^g, a minimal init.ora is very brief. One of the major goals in this new version is to simplify the DBA's tasks as much as possible. A typical minimal init.ora file for Oracle 10^g might be:

```
COMPATIBLE=10.1.0.1.0
DB_BLOCK_SIZE=16384
DB_CREATE_FILE_DEST=/db1/oradata
```

```
DB_CREATE_ONLINE_LOG_DEST_1=/db2/oradata

DB_NAME=orcl

DB_RECOVERY_FILE_DEST=/db3/oradata/flash_recovery_area

DB_RECOVERY_FILE_DEST_SIZE=2048M

PGA_AGGREGATE_TARGET=80M

SGA_TARGET=200M

UNDO_MANAGEMENT=AUTO

BACKGROUND_DUMP_DEST=?/admin/orcl/bdump

CORE_DUMP_DEST=?/admin/orcl/cdump

USER_DUMP_DEST=?/admin/orcl/udump
```

In Oracle 9*i*, the minimal version has a few more parameters related to the system global area (SGA), but only a single additional total parameter since it doesn't support the **DB_RECOVERY_FILE_DEST** parameters of 10^g.

```
COMPATIBLE=9.2.0.4.0

DB_BLOCK_SIZE=16384

DB_CREATE_FILE_DEST=/db1/oradata

DB_CREATE_ONLINE_LOG_DEST_1=/db2/oradata

DB_NAME=orcl

DB_CACHE_SIZE=100M

JAVA_POOL_SIZE=50M
```

```
LARGE_POOL_SIZE=10M
SHARED_POOL_SIZE=50M
PGA_AGGREGATE_TARGET=80M
UNDO_MANAGEMENT=AUTO
BACKGROUND_DUMP_DEST=?/admin/orcl/bdump
CORE_DUMP_DEST=?/admin/orcl/cdump
USER_DUMP_DEST=?/admin/orcl/udump
```

The two main differences between a 10^g init.ora and a 9*i* init.ora are the RMAN parameters DB_RECOVERY_FILE_DEST and DB_RECOVERY_FILE_DEST_SIZE, which are now available in 10^g, and the SGA_TARGET parameter, which is not supported in 9*i*. For 9*i*, you must set DB_CACHE_SIZE, JAVA_POOL_SIZE, LARGE_POOL_SIZE, and SHARED_POOL_SIZE rather than just the single SGA_TARGET parameter.

Setting Up the Environment

In UNIX, all Oracle environment settings are done with environment variables. Setting up an environment for a new database consists of just a few simple commands. Oracle has created some shell scripts and a configuration file to assist you in setting the proper environment variables. The "oratab" file is located in either /etc/oratab or /var/opt/oracle/oratab, depending on what flavor of UNIX you're using. Many DBAs use a symlink to make it always available as /etc/oratab, simplifying scripting. In Korn shell (ksh), a complete example is:

```
echo "orcl:/home/oracle/10.1.0:N" >>/etc/oratab
export ORAENV_ASK=NO
export ORACLE_SID=orcl
. oraenv
```

As is frequently the case, things are a bit more complicated in Windows. The ORACLE_SID variable mentioned above can be set in the Windows Registry, as well as in an environment variable. The Registry key in question is also called ORACLE_SID, and is a string value stored in:

HKEY_LOCAL_MACHINE\SOFTWARE\ORACLE\HOME0

The number at the end of the above string might change if you have more than one ORACLE_HOME directory on the system in question. The first home uses HOME0, the second HOME1, and so on. If no databases have been previously created in a home, the ORACLE_SID string may not be present. If not, it's okay to create it. The ORACLE_SID defined in the Registry is the default one for that ORACLE_HOME, and will always be used if no value is specified in an environment variable.

Normally, you do not have to manually manipulate the Registry since Oracle's ORADIM utility generally handles it correctly. Before you can create a new database on Windows, you must first create a service so that the database can start and run in the background, with no user logged in. The syntax to create a new database service is:

```
oradim.exe -new -sid ORCL -startmode a
```

The above command creates a new database service and sets it to start automatically every time the system is booted. You can also start, stop, and delete database services with the ORADIM command. Examples, in order, are:

```
oradim.exe -startup -sid ORCL
oradim.exe -shutdown -sid ORCL
oradim.exe -delete -sid ORCL
```

After using ORADIM to delete a database service, no ORACLE_SID will be set in the Registry since it gets deleted along with the database service.

Connect to the Database as SYSDBA

Once the environment has been set up properly, the next step is to connect to the currently non-existent database with enough privilege to create the database. This step is the same on both Windows and UNIX.

```
sqlplus /nolog
connect / as sysdba
startup nomount
```

The second and third commands are typed at the "SQL>" prompt, inside SQL Plus.

Issue the "Create Database" Command

At this point, you are now ready to actually create the database. Both of the init.ora examples listed previously are configured to use Oracle-managed files (OMFs), which lets Oracle automatically locate, name, size, and resize datafiles. Given that, the minimal "create database" command requires just three words:

```
create database ORCL;
```

Since the database has been configured to use OMF and has automatic undo management, this command will create the system tablespace, an undo tablespace, redo logs, and control files. In Oracle 10^g, a temporary tablespace and a tablespace named SYSAUX will also be created.

A slightly more complete version of the "create database" command is:

```
create database ORCL
    datafile size 300M autoextend on next 10M maxsize unlimited
    extent management local
    sysaux datafile size 120M autoextend on next 10M maxsize unlimited
    default temporary tablespace temp tempfile size 20M autoextend on next 5M
        maxsize unlimited extent management local
    undo tablespace undotbs1 datafile size 200M autoextend on next 5M maxsize
unlimited
    user sys identified by syspass
```

```
user system identified by systempass
character set AL32UTF8
national character set AL16UTF16
logfile group 1 size 10M, group 2 size 10M, group 3 size 10M;
```

The above example is for 10*g*, but could easily be adapted for 9*i* by removing the entire line that begins with "sysaux". Even with OMF turned on, filenames can be explicitly specified for any datafile, even the ones in the create database statement.

Create Additional Tablespaces

A database with nothing but the required minimum number of tablespaces is not very useful. To create additional tablespaces, use the "create tablespace" command:

```
create tablespace data01 datafile size 500M autoextend on next 50M maxsize
unlimited
    extent management local uniform size 5M segment space management auto;

create tablespace index01 datafile '/db1/oradata/orcl/index01_01.dbf' size 500M
    extent management local autoallocate segment space management auto;
```

The first example command creates a tablespace called "data01" and lets OMF take care of locating and naming the file. The second command specifies the filename explicitly.

Run Data Dictionary Scripts

Before the database can be used for anything other than file management, the data dictionary must be created. A minimal database requires two scripts: catalog.sql and catproc.sql. They must be run in order, with catalog.sql first and catproc.sql second. The scripts can be found in $ORACLE_HOME/rdbms/admin, and you must be connected as SYSDBA to run them.

Run Additional Dictionary Scripts

If any optional Oracle features such as Java stored procedures are to be used, additional dictionary scripts should be run at this time. Each optional component will have at least one script to be run. Please see the documentation for a component to determine exactly what to run. In Oracle 9i, many of the optional components will also require additional tablespaces with specific names.

Automating the "Manual" Process

Even without using the DBCA, the entire database creation can be automated. A sample script for UNIX is:

```
#!/bin/ksh
#### begin create_orcl.sh ####
# This is a korn shell script.
```

```
# Set up environment.
echo "orcl:/home/oracle/10.1.0:N" >>/etc/oratab
export ORAENV_ASK=NO
export ORACLE_SID=orcl
. oraenv

# Create necessary directories.
mkdir -p /db1/oradata
mkdir -p /db2/oradata
mkdir -p /db3/oradata/flash_recovery_area
mkdir -p $ORACLE_HOME/admin/orcl
mkdir $ORACLE_HOME/admin/orcl/archive
mkdir $ORACLE_HOME/admin/orcl/bdump
mkdir $ORACLE_HOME/admin/orcl/cdump
mkdir $ORACLE_HOME/admin/orcl/udump

# Copy the init.ora to the dbs directory.
cp init.ora $ORACLE_HOME/dbs/initorcl.ora

# Run the database creation SQL.
sqlplus /nolog @create_orcl.sql
```

```
#### end create_orcl.sh ####

---- begin create_orcl.sql ----
spool create_orcl.log
whenever sqlerror exit 1

connect / as sysdba

-- Create a server parameter file from the init.ora.
create spfile from pfile;

startup nomount

create database ORCL
    datafile size 300M autoextend on next 10M maxsize unlimited
    extent management local
    sysaux datafile size 120M autoextend on next 10M maxsize unlimited
    default temporary tablespace temp tempfile size 20M autoextend on next 5M
       maxsize unlimited extent management local
    undo tablespace undotbs1 datafile size 200M autoextend on next 5M maxsize
unlimited
    user sys identified by syspass
```

```
user system identified by systempass
character set AL32UTF8
national character set AL16UTF16
logfile group 1 size 10M, group 2 size 10M, group 3 size 10M;

create tablespace data01 datafile size 500M autoextend on next 50M maxsize unlim-
ited
    extent management local uniform size 5M segment space management auto;

create tablespace index01 datafile size 500M autoextend on next 50M maxsize
unlimited
    extent management local uniform size 5M segment space management auto;


@?/rdbms/admin/catalog
@?/rdbms/admin/catproc


exit
---- create_orcl.sql ----
```

AUTOMATING DATABASE DELETION WITHOUT THE DBCA

In Oracle 10^g, an automated database deletion script looks like this:

```
shutdown immediate;
startup restrict mount;
drop database;
```

To run the script, start SQL Plus, connect as sysdba, and run the three commands. On Windows, you'll need to use ORADIM to delete the database service afterward as well.

```
oradim.exe -delete -sid ORCL
```

Things are more involved in 9i because there's no drop command for the database. Because of this, you'll need to query the database to find all data, temp, and control files, plus all redo logs. A SQL script to generate a file deletion script is:

```
set echo off feedback off head off pagesize 0 linesize 200 trimspool on

spool rm_db_files.sh

select 'rm '||name from v$controlfile
```

```
union
select 'rm '||member from v$logfile
union
select 'rm '||name from v$tempfile
union
select 'rm '||name from v$datafile
select 'rm '||value from v$parameter
where name in ('pfile','spfile','ifile')
/

spool off
exit
```

Running the above SQL generates a shell script named rm_db_files.sh, which can be run to delete all the important files belonging to this database. Before running the script, the database should be shut down and, if on Windows, the database service should be removed with ORADIM.

REFERENCE

DBCA Command Line Parameters

The DBCA tool supports the command line parameters described in Table 3-1. Use "dbca -help" for more syntax definition.

Table 3-1 DBCA Command Line Parameters

Parameter	Purpose	Additional Comments
-silent	Instructs the DBCA to run a silent session.	Mutually exclusive with -progress_only.
-progress_only	Instructs the DBCA to run a silent session, except for displaying a progress dialog during database creation.	Mutually exclusive with -silent.
-responseFile <filename>	Tells the DBCA which response file, if any, to use.	A filename of NO_VALUE can be used to indicate no response file.

Table 3-1 DBCA Command Line Parameters (continued)

Parameter	Purpose	Additional Comments
-continueOnNonFatalErrors <value>	Instructs the DBCA to continue past ignorable errors.	Valid values are TRUE and FALSE.
-createDatabase	Tells the DBCA that this is a database creation session.	
-templateName <name>	Identifies which template to use for creating a new database or new template.	Should not be a fully qualified name. All templates are used from, or created in, the DBCA templates directory.
-gdbName <global DB name>	Specifies a global name for the database being created.	If using a DB_DOMAIN, this should generally be DB_NAME||'.'||DB_DOMAIN.
-sid <sid>	Specifies a SID for the database being created.	Equal to DB_NAME.

Table 3-1   DBCA Command Line Parameters (continued)

Parameter	Purpose	Additional Comments
-dbsnmpPassword <password> -sysPassword <password> -systemPassword <password> -sysmanPassword <password>	Provides non-default passwords for the dbsnmp, sys, system, and sysman accounts, respectively.	If no password is specified for a given account, the traditional defaults will be used. dbsnmp and sysman passwords should only be provided when emConfiguration is specified.
-emConfiguration <config type>	Tells the DBCA if it should configure the new database for use with Oracle Enterprise Manager.	Valid config types are LOCAL, CENTRAL, NOBACKUP, NOEMAIL, and NONE.
-hostUserName <os username> -hostPassword <os password>	Provides an operating system username and password to the DBCA.	Only used when emConfiguration is specified with some configuration type other than NOBACKUP or NONE.

Table 3-1   DBCA Command Line Parameters (continued)

Parameter	Purpose	Additional Comments
`-backupSchedule <backup time>`	Specifies the time for which the DBCA should schedule a daily backup.	Time should be in the form HH24:MM. Only used when emConfiguration is specified with some configuration type other than NOBACKUP or NONE.
`-smtpServer <host>`	Identifies hostname or IP address to be used for sending email.	Only used when emConfiguration is specified with some configuration type other than NOEMAIL or NONE.
`-emailAddress <address>`	Identifies email address that should receive emailed alerts.	Only used when emConfiguration is specified with some configuration type other than NOEMAIL or NONE.

Table 3-1 DBCA Command Line Parameters *(continued)*

Parameter	Purpose	Additional Comments
-centralAgent <agent location>	Identifies centralized EM agent location.	Only used when emConfiguration is specified with a configuration type of CENTRAL.
-datafileDestination <directory>	Specifies a destination directory for all database files.	Should be a fully qualified directory name.
-datafileNames <filename>	Specifies a text file, consisting of name=value pairs, specifying mappings from datafiles to raw device names.	Should be a fully qualified filename.
-recoveryAreaDestination <directory>	Specifies the location of the flashback recovery area for the database being created.	Should be a fully qualified directory name.
-datafileJarLocation <directory>	Tells the DBCA where to find the jar file containing the database files that go with the specified template.	This directive specifies a directory name, not a file. The directory name should be fully qualified.

Table 3-1 DBCA Command Line Parameters (continued)

Parameter	Purpose	Additional Comments
-characterSet <char set identifier>	Specifies the database's main character set.	Example value: AL32UTF8.
-nationalCharacterSet <char set id>	Specifies the database's alternate character set.	Example value: AL16UTF16.
-registerWithDirService <value>	Tells the DBCA if it should register this database with a directory service (Lightweight Directory Access Protocol [LDAP]) or not.	Valid values are TRUE and FALSE.
-dirServiceUserName <username> -dirServicePassword <password>	Provides username and password to use when-registering the new database with a directory service.	Useful only when -registerWithDirService is TRUE.
-walletPassword <password>	Specifies database wallet password.	Useful only when -registerWithDirService is TRUE.

Table 3-1 DBCA Command Line Parameters (continued)

Parameter	Purpose	Additional Comments
-listeners <listener list>	Provides the names of one or more listeners with which the new database should register.	If this parameter is not specified, the database will register with all listeners on the local host.
-variablesFile <filename>	Specifies the name of a file containing name=value pairs.	Used to set the DBCA variables, such as ORACLE_BASE and DB_NAME.
-storageType <value>	Tells the DBCA what type of disk storage to use for the new database.	Valid values are FS, RAW, and ASM. FS selects filesystem (normal) storage, RAW specifies raw filesystems, and ASM indicates that 10^g's new automatic storage management facility is to be used.

Table 3-1 DBCA Command Line Parameters *(continued)*

Parameter	Purpose	Additional Comments
-diskList <list>	List of disks to be used with Automatic Storage Management (ASM).	Only useful when -storageType ASM is indicated.
-diskGroupName <name>	When using ASM, this parameter tells the DBCA what to name the ASM group it creates.	Only useful when -storageType ASM is indicated.
-diskString <path>	ASM disk discovery path.	Only useful when -storageType ASM is indicated.
-asmPassword <password>	SYS password for ASM instance.	Only useful when -storageType ASM is indicated.
-createTemplateFromDB	Tells the DBCA that this is a database template creation session.	This operation will create a template based on a running database.

Table 3-1 DBCA Command Line Parameters (continued)

Parameter	Purpose	Additional Comments
-sourceDB <host>:<port>:<sid>	Specifies which database will be used for the template source.	This variation of sourceDB is used only with createTemplateFromDB.
-sysDBAUserName <username> -sysDBAPassword <password>	Specifies the sys username and password for the template source database.	
-maintainFileLocations <value>	Tells the DBCA if it should maintain the database's current file paths or change them to conform with OFA.	Valid values are TRUE and FALSE.
-createCloneTemplate	Tells the DBCA that this is a database clone creation session.	This operation will create a database template, plus a jarred set of datafiles based on a running database.
-sourceDB <sid>	Specifies which database will be used for the clone source.	This variation of sourceDB is used only with createCloneTemplate.

Table 3-1 DBCA Command Line Parameters *(continued)*

Parameter	Purpose	Additional Comments
-generateScripts	Tells the DBCA that this is a database script generation session.	
-scriptDest <directory>	Specifies destination directory for database scripts.	Should be a fully qualified directory name.
-deleteDatabase	Tells the DBCA that this is a database deletion session.	
-help	Tells the DBCA to print a list of command line parameters, along with brief descriptions, then exit.	

Response File Syntax

DBCA response files are plain text files. Installer settings are specified as name/value pairs in the following form:

<name> = <value>

<name> is always a single string, with no spaces, and is case-insensitive.

<value> can be a number, Boolean, string, or string list. The different value types are represented as shown in Table 3-2:

Table 3-2   Value Types Supported by DBCA Response Files

Type	Example
Number	99
Boolean*	TRUE
String	"Sample string"
String List	{ "string1", "string2" }

* Boolean values are completely case-insensitive.

In both Oracle 10g and Oracle 9i, the response file is organized in sections, similar to old-style Windows ".ini" files. Each section has specific set of allowable keywords and values. The sections are shown in Table 3-3:

Table 3-3 DBCA Response File Sections

Section Name	Purpose
General	Contains the version number of the response file, and the create type.
createDatabase	Contains information needed to run a database creation session.
createTemplateFromDB	Contains information needed to run a database template creation session.
createCloneTemplate	Contains information needed to run a clone creation session.
deleteDatabase	Contains information needed to run a database deletion session.
generateScripts	Contains information needed to run a script generation session.

A response file can also contain comments. A comment is any line that begins with the # character. The supported syntax for the DBCA response files, by section, is shown in Table 3-4:

Table 3-4   Supported Syntax, by Section

Name	Value Type	Description
[General] Section		
RESPONSEFILE_VERSION	String	Response file version number. For the DBCA, this should match the major version of the database being used. Oracle 9*i* Release 2 would use "9.2", for example.
CREATE_TYPE	String	Tells the DBCA what type of response file to expect. Valid values are "createDatabase", "createTemplateFromDB", "createCloneTemplate", "deleteDatabase", and "generateScripts".
[createDatabase] Section		
GDBNAME	String	Specifies a global name for the database being created.
SID	String	Specifies a SID for the database being created.

Table 3-4 Supported Syntax, by Section *(continued)*

Name	Value Type	Description
TEMPLATENAME	String	Designates which database template to use. This is not a filename, but must match a template name as it appears in the DBCA. This name is found in the <DatabaseTemplate name="" > tag of the template file.
DATAFILEJARLOCATION	String	Tells the DBCA where to find the jar file containing the database files that go with the specified template.
DATAFILEDESTINATION	String	Specifies a destination directory for all database files.
CHARACTERSET	String	Specifies the database's main character set.
NATIONALCHARACTERSET	String	Specifies the database's alternate character set.
REGISTERWITHDIRSERVICE	Boolean	Tells the DBCA if it should register this database with a directory service (LDAP) or not.
DIRESERVICEUSERNAME	String	Provides username to use when registering the new database with a directory service.
DIRSERVICEPASSWORD	String	Provides password to use when registering the new database with a directory service.

Table 3-4 Supported Syntax, by Section (continued)

Name	Value Type	Description
LISTENERS	String	Space-separated string that provides the names of one or more listeners with which the new database should register.
VARIABLESFILE	String	Specifies the name of a file containing name=value pairs, which is used to set DBCA variables such as ORACLE_BASE and DB_NAME.
STORAGETYPE	String	Tells the DBCA what type of disk storage to use for the new database. Valid values are FS, RAW, and ASM. FS selects filesystem (normal) storage, RAW specifies raw filesystems, and ASM indicates that $10g$'s new automatic storage management facility is to be used.
DISKLIST	String	Comma-separated list of disks to be used with ASM.
DISKGROUPNAME	String	When using ASM, this parameter tells the DBCA what to name the ASM group it creates.

Table 3-4 Supported Syntax, by Section (continued)

Name	Value Type	Description
[createTemplateFromDB] Section		
SOURCEDB	String	Specifies which database will be used for the template source. String should be in the form "<host>:<port>:<SID>".
SYSDBAUSERNAME	String	Specifies the sys username for the template source database.
SYSDBAPASSWORD	String	Specifies the sys password for the template source database.
TEMPLATENAME	String	Specifies the filename (not fully qualified) of the template to be generated.
[createCloneTemplate] Section		
SOURCEDB	String	Specifies the SID of the local database to be used for the template source. String should be in the form "<SID>".
SYSDBAUSERNAME	String	Specifies the sys username for the template source database.
SYSDBAPASSWORD	String	Specifies the sys password for the template source database.
TEMPLATENAME	String	Specifies the filename (not fully qualified) of the template to be generated.

Table 3-4 Supported Syntax, by Section (continued)

Name	Value Type	Description
DATAFILEJARLOCATION	String	Tells the DBCA where to create the jar file containing the database files to go with the new template.
[deleteDatabase] Section		
SOURCEDB	String	Specifies the SID of the local database to be deleted. String should be in the form "<SID>".
SYSDBAUSERNAME	String	Specifies the sys username of the database to be deleted.
SYSDBAPASSWORD	String	Specifies the sys password of the database to be deleted.
[generateScripts] Section		
TEMPLATENAME	String	Designates the database template to be used. This is not a filename, but must match a template name as it appears in the DBCA. This name is found in the <DatabaseTemplate name=""> tag of the template file.
GDBNAME	String	Specifies a global name for the database being created.
SCRIPTDESTINATION	String	Specifies the destination directory for database scripts.

SAMPLE DBCA RESPONSE FILE

```
# Custom DBCA response file

# Creates a new database based on

# the general-purpose template.

[GENERAL]

RESPONSEFILE_VERSION = "10.0.0"

CREATE_TYPE = "createDatabase"


[CREATEDATABASE]

GDBNAME = "orcl.domain.com"

SID = "orcl"

TEMPLATENAME = "General Purpose"

#DATAFILEJARLOCATION =

DATAFILEDESTINATION = "C:\oracle\ora10"

CHARACTERSET = "AL32UTF8"

NATIONALCHARACTERSET= "UTF8"

#REGISTERWITHDIRSERVICE= TRUE

#DIRSERVICEUSERNAME= "name"

#DIRSERVICEPASSWORD= "password"
```

```
#LISTENERS = "listener1 listener2"

#VARIABLESFILE =

STORAGETYPE=FS

#DISKLIST=disk1,disk2

#DISKGROUPNAME=DATA
```

SAMPLE DATABASE TEMPLATE

```
<DatabaseTemplate name="orcl" description="" version="10.0.0.0">
  <CommonAttributes>
    <option name="ISEARCH" value="false"/>
    <option name="OMS" value="false"/>
    <option name="JSERVER" value="true"/>
    <option name="SPATIAL" value="false"/>
    <option name="ODM" value="false">
      <tablespace id="SYSAUX"/>
    </option>
    <option name="IMEDIA" value="false"/>
    <option name="XDB_PROTOCOLS" value="false">
      <tablespace id="SYSAUX"/>
```

```
      </option>
      <option name="ORACLE_TEXT" value="false">
         <tablespace id="SYSAUX"/>
      </option>
      <option name="SAMPLE_SCHEMA" value="false">
         <tablespace id="EXAMPLE"/>
      </option>
      <option name="CWMLITE" value="false">
         <tablespace id="SYSAUX"/>
      </option>
      <option name="EM_REPOSITORY" value="true">
         <tablespace id="SYSAUX"/>
      </option>
   </CommonAttributes>
   <Variables/>
   <CustomScripts Execute="false"/>
   <InitParamAttributes>
      <InitParams>
         <initParam name="pga_aggregate_target" value="24" unit="MB"/>
         <initParam name="sort_area_size" value="65536"/>
```

```
        <initParam name="log_archive_dest_1" value="'LOCA-
TION={ORACLE_BASE}\admin\{DB_NAME}\archive'"/>
        <initParam name="processes" value="150"/>
        <initParam name="db_create_online_log_dest_1"
value="{ORACLE_BASE}\admin\{DB_NAME}\oradata1"/>
        <initParam name="db_recovery_file_dest_size" value="2048" unit="MB"/>
        <initParam name="sga_target" value="160" unit="MB"/>
        <initParam name="compatible" value="10.1.0.1.0"/>
        <initParam name="db_create_file_dest"
value="{ORACLE_BASE}\admin\{DB_NAME}\oradata"/>
        <initParam name="background_dump_dest"
value="{ORACLE_BASE}\admin\{DB_NAME}\bdump"/>
        <initParam name="job_queue_processes" value="2"/>
        <initParam name="db_name" value="orcl"/>
        <initParam name="user_dump_dest"
value="{ORACLE_BASE}\admin\{DB_NAME}\udump"/>
        <initParam name="db_domain" value=""/>
        <initParam name="open_cursors" value="300"/>
        <initParam name="db_block_size" value="8" unit="KB"/>
        <initParam name="db_recovery_file_dest"
value="{ORACLE_BASE}\admin\{DB_NAME}\flash_recovery_area"/>
        <initParam name="undo_tablespace" value="UNDOTBS1"/>
```

```xml
        <initParam name="log_archive_format" value="%t_%s_%r.dbf"/>
        <initParam name="core_dump_dest"
value="{ORACLE_BASE}\admin\{DB_NAME}\cdump"/>
        <initParam name="remote_login_passwordfile" value="EXCLUSIVE"/>
        <initParam name="undo_management" value="AUTO"/>
        <initParam name="db_file_multiblock_read_count" value="16"/>
    </InitParams>
    <MiscParams>
        <databaseType>MULTIPURPOSE</databaseType>
        <maxUserConn>20</maxUserConn>
        <percentageMemTOSGA>40</percentageMemTOSGA>
        <customSGA>true</customSGA>
        <characterSet>AL32UTF8</characterSet>
        <nationalCharacterSet>AL16UTF16</nationalCharacterSet>
        <archiveLogMode>true</archiveLogMode>
        <initParamFileName>{ORACLE_BASE}\admin\{DB_NAME}\pfile\init.ora</init-
ParamFileName>
    </MiscParams>
    <SPfile useSPfile="true">{ORACLE_HOME}\database\spfile{SID}.ora</SPfile>
</InitParamAttributes>
<StorageAttributes>
```

```
<ControlfileAttributes id="Controlfile">
  <maxDatafiles>100</maxDatafiles>
  <maxLogfiles>16</maxLogfiles>
  <maxLogMembers>3</maxLogMembers>
  <maxLogHistory>1</maxLogHistory>
  <maxInstances>8</maxInstances>
  <image name="&lt;OMF_CONTROL_0="  filepath="{ORACLE_BASE}\orad-
ata\{DB_NAME}\"/>
  <image name="&lt;OMF_CONTROL_1="  filepath="{ORACLE_BASE}\orad-
ata\{DB_NAME}\"/>
  <image name="&lt;OMF_CONTROL_2="  filepath="{ORACLE_BASE}\orad-
ata\{DB_NAME}\"/>
</ControlfileAttributes>
<DatafileAttributes id="&lt;OMF_EXAMPLE_DATAFILE_0_>">
  <tablespace>EXAMPLE</tablespace>
  <temporary>false</temporary>
  <online>true</online>
  <status>0</status>
  <size unit="MB">150</size>
  <reuse>true</reuse>
  <autoExtend>true</autoExtend>
```

```
        <increment unit="KB">640</increment>
        <maxSize unit="MB">-1</maxSize>
    </DatafileAttributes>
    <DatafileAttributes id="&lt;OMF_SYSAUX_DATAFILE_0>">
        <tablespace>SYSAUX</tablespace>
        <temporary>false</temporary>
        <online>true</online>
        <status>0</status>
        <size unit="MB">120</size>
        <reuse>true</reuse>
        <autoExtend>true</autoExtend>
        <increment unit="KB">10240</increment>
        <maxSize unit="MB">-1</maxSize>
    </DatafileAttributes>
    <DatafileAttributes id="&lt;OMF_SYSTEM_DATAFILE_0>">
        <tablespace>SYSTEM</tablespace>
        <temporary>false</temporary>
        <online>true</online>
        <status>0</status>
        <size unit="MB">300</size>
        <reuse>true</reuse>
```

```
<autoExtend>true</autoExtend>
<increment unit="KB">10240</increment>
<maxSize unit="MB">-1</maxSize>
</DatafileAttributes>
<DatafileAttributes id="&lt;OMF_TEMP_DATAFILE_0>">
<tablespace>TEMP</tablespace>
<temporary>false</temporary>
<online>true</online>
<status>0</status>
<size unit="MB">20</size>
<reuse>true</reuse>
<autoExtend>true</autoExtend>
<increment unit="KB">640</increment>
<maxSize unit="MB">-1</maxSize>
</DatafileAttributes>
<DatafileAttributes id="&lt;OMF_UNDOTBS1_DATAFILE_0>">
<tablespace>UNDOTBS1</tablespace>
<temporary>false</temporary>
<online>true</online>
<status>0</status>
<size unit="MB">200</size>
```

```xml
        <reuse>true</reuse>
        <autoExtend>true</autoExtend>
        <increment unit="KB">5120</increment>
        <maxSize unit="MB">-1</maxSize>
      </DatafileAttributes>
      <DatafileAttributes id="&lt;OMF_USERS_DATAFILE_0>">
        <tablespace>USERS</tablespace>
        <temporary>false</temporary>
        <online>true</online>
        <status>0</status>
        <size unit="MB">5</size>
        <reuse>true</reuse>
        <autoExtend>true</autoExtend>
        <increment unit="KB">1280</increment>
        <maxSize unit="MB">-1</maxSize>
      </DatafileAttributes>
      <TablespaceAttributes id="EXAMPLE">
        <online>true</online>
        <offlineMode>1</offlineMode>
        <readOnly>false</readOnly>
        <temporary>false</temporary>
```

```
<defaultTemp>false</defaultTemp>
<undo>false</undo>
<local>true</local>
<blockSize>-1</blockSize>
<allocation>1</allocation>
<uniAllocSize unit="KB">-1</uniAllocSize>
<initSize unit="KB">64</initSize>
<increment unit="KB">64</increment>
<incrementPercent>50</incrementPercent>
<minExtends>1</minExtends>
<maxExtends>4096</maxExtends>
<minExtendsSize unit="KB">64</minExtendsSize>
<logging>true</logging>
<recoverable>false</recoverable>
<maxFreeSpace>0</maxFreeSpace>
<autoSegmentMgmt>true</autoSegmentMgmt>
<datafilesList>
    <TablespaceDatafileAttributes id="&lt;OMF_EXAMPLE_DATAFILE_0>">
        <id>-1</id>
    </TablespaceDatafileAttributes>
</datafilesList>
```

```
</TablespaceAttributes>
<TablespaceAttributes id="SYSAUX">
<online>true</online>
<offlineMode>1</offlineMode>
<readOnly>false</readOnly>
<temporary>false</temporary>
<defaultTemp>false</defaultTemp>
<undo>false</undo>
<local>true</local>
<blockSize>-1</blockSize>
<allocation>1</allocation>
<uniAllocSize unit="KB">-1</uniAllocSize>
<initSize unit="KB">64</initSize>
<increment unit="KB">64</increment>
<incrementPercent>50</incrementPercent>
<minExtends>1</minExtends>
<maxExtends>4096</maxExtends>
<minExtendsSize unit="KB">64</minExtendsSize>
<logging>true</logging>
<recoverable>false</recoverable>
<maxFreeSpace>0</maxFreeSpace>
```

```
<autoSegmentMgmt>true</autoSegmentMgmt>
<datafilesList>
   <TablespaceDatafileAttributes id="&lt;OMF_SYSAUX_DATAFILE_0>">
      <id>-1</id>
   </TablespaceDatafileAttributes>
</datafilesList>
</TablespaceAttributes>
<TablespaceAttributes id="SYSTEM">
<online>true</online>
<offlineMode>1</offlineMode>
<readOnly>false</readOnly>
<temporary>false</temporary>
<defaultTemp>false</defaultTemp>
<undo>false</undo>
<local>true</local>
<blockSize>-1</blockSize>
<allocation>3</allocation>
<uniAllocSize unit="KB">-1</uniAllocSize>
<initSize unit="KB">64</initSize>
<increment unit="KB">64</increment>
<incrementPercent>50</incrementPercent>
```

```xml
<minExtends>1</minExtends>
<maxExtends>-1</maxExtends>
<minExtendsSize unit="KB">64</minExtendsSize>
<logging>true</logging>
<recoverable>false</recoverable>
<maxFreeSpace>0</maxFreeSpace>
<autoSegmentMgmt>true</autoSegmentMgmt>
<datafilesList>
    <TablespaceDatafileAttributes id="&lt;OMF_SYSTEM_DATAFILE_0>">
        <id>-1</id>
    </TablespaceDatafileAttributes>
</datafilesList>
</TablespaceAttributes>
<TablespaceAttributes id="TEMP">
<online>true</online>
<offlineMode>1</offlineMode>
<readOnly>false</readOnly>
<temporary>true</temporary>
<defaultTemp>true</defaultTemp>
<undo>false</undo>
<local>true</local>
```

```
<blockSize>-1</blockSize>
<allocation>1</allocation>
<uniAllocSize unit="KB">-1</uniAllocSize>
<initSize unit="KB">64</initSize>
<increment unit="KB">64</increment>
<incrementPercent>0</incrementPercent>
<minExtends>1</minExtends>
<maxExtends>0</maxExtends>
<minExtendsSize unit="KB">64</minExtendsSize>
<logging>true</logging>
<recoverable>false</recoverable>
<maxFreeSpace>0</maxFreeSpace>
<autoSegmentMgmt>true</autoSegmentMgmt>
<datafilesList>
   <TablespaceDatafileAttributes id="&lt;OMF_TEMP_DATAFILE_0>">
      <id>-1</id>
   </TablespaceDatafileAttributes>
</datafilesList>
</TablespaceAttributes>
<TablespaceAttributes id="UNDOTBS1">
<online>true</online>
```

```
<offlineMode>1</offlineMode>
<readOnly>false</readOnly>
<temporary>false</temporary>
<defaultTemp>false</defaultTemp>
<undo>true</undo>
<local>true</local>
<blockSize>-1</blockSize>
<allocation>1</allocation>
<uniAllocSize unit="KB">-1</uniAllocSize>
<initSize unit="KB">512</initSize>
<increment unit="KB">512</increment>
<incrementPercent>50</incrementPercent>
<minExtends>8</minExtends>
<maxExtends>4096</maxExtends>
<minExtendsSize unit="KB">512</minExtendsSize>
<logging>true</logging>
<recoverable>false</recoverable>
<maxFreeSpace>0</maxFreeSpace>
<autoSegmentMgmt>true</autoSegmentMgmt>
<datafilesList>
    <TablespaceDatafileAttributes id="&lt;OMF_UNDOTBS1_DATAFILE_0>">
```

```
              <id>-1</id>
            </TablespaceDatafileAttributes>
          </datafilesList>
        </TablespaceAttributes>
        <TablespaceAttributes id="USERS">
          <online>true</online>
          <offlineMode>1</offlineMode>
          <readOnly>false</readOnly>
          <temporary>false</temporary>
          <defaultTemp>false</defaultTemp>
          <undo>false</undo>
          <local>true</local>
          <blockSize>-1</blockSize>
          <allocation>1</allocation>
          <uniAllocSize unit="KB">-1</uniAllocSize>
          <initSize unit="KB">128</initSize>
          <increment unit="KB">128</increment>
          <incrementPercent>0</incrementPercent>
          <minExtends>1</minExtends>
          <maxExtends>4096</maxExtends>
          <minExtendsSize unit="KB">128</minExtendsSize>
```

```xml
<logging>true</logging>
<recoverable>false</recoverable>
<maxFreeSpace>0</maxFreeSpace>
<autoSegmentMgmt>true</autoSegmentMgmt>
<datafilesList>
  <TablespaceDatafileAttributes id="&lt;OMF_USERS_DATAFILE_0>">
    <id>-1</id>
  </TablespaceDatafileAttributes>
</datafilesList>
</TablespaceAttributes>
<RedoLogGroupAttributes id="1">
<reuse>false</reuse>
<fileSize unit="KB">10240</fileSize>
<Thread>1</Thread>
<member ordinal="0" memberName="OMF_1_REDOLOG_MEMBER_0" file-
path="{ORACLE_BASE}\oradata\{DB_NAME}\"/>
</RedoLogGroupAttributes>
<RedoLogGroupAttributes id="2">
<reuse>false</reuse>
<fileSize unit="KB">10240</fileSize>
<Thread>1</Thread>
```

```
            <member ordinal="0" memberName="OMF_2_REDOLOG_MEMBER_0" file-
path="{ORACLE_BASE}\oradata\{DB_NAME}\"/>
          </RedoLogGroupAttributes>
          <RedoLogGroupAttributes id="3">
            <reuse>false</reuse>
            <fileSize unit="KB">10240</fileSize>
            <Thread>1</Thread>
            <member ordinal="0" memberName="OMF_3_REDOLOG_MEMBER_0" file-
path="{ORACLE_BASE}\oradata\{DB_NAME}\"/>
          </RedoLogGroupAttributes>
      </StorageAttributes>
    </DatabaseTemplate>
```

BASIC INITIALIZATION (INIT.ORA) PARAMETERS

This section defines some of the most common and/or important initialization parameters. Each parameter is in its own section, and each section begins with a table of the properties of the parameter and has a description of how the parameter is used following the table.

BACKGROUND_DUMP_DEST

Table 3-5 BACKGROUND_DUMP_DEST

Property	Description
Parameter type	String
Syntax	BACKGROUND_DUMP_DEST = { *pathname* | *directory* }
Default value	OS-dependent
Modifiable	ALTER SYSTEM
Range of values	Any valid local path, directory, or disk

BACKGROUND_DUMP_DEST specifies the pathname (directory or disc) where debugging trace files for the background processes (LGWR, DBWn, and so on) are written during Oracle operations.

An alert file in the directory specified by BACKGROUND_DUMP_DEST logs significant database events and messages. Anything that affects the database instance or global database is recorded here. The alert file is a normal text file. Its filename is operating system dependent. For platforms that support multiple instances, it takes the form alert_sid.log, where sid is the system identifier. This file grows slowly, but without limit, so you might want to delete it periodically. You can delete the file even when the database is running.

CLUSTER_DATABASE

Table 3-6   CLUSTER_DATABASE

Property	Description
Parameter type	Boolean
Default value	FALSE
Modifiable	No
Range of values	TRUE l FALSE
Real Application Clusters	Multiple instances must have the same value

CLUSTER_DATABASE is a Real Application Clusters parameter that specifies whether or not the Real Application Clusters feature is enabled.

COMPATIBLE

Table 3-7 COMPATIBLE

Property	Description
Parameter type	String
Syntax	COMPATIBLE = *release_number*
Default value	9.0.0 (for 9i) or 10.0.0 (for 10g)
Modifiable	No
Range of values	9.0.0 to default release
Real Application Clusters	Multiple instances must have the same value

COMPATIBLE allows you to use a new release of Oracle, while at the same time guaranteeing backward compatibility with an earlier release. This is helpful if it becomes necessary to revert to the earlier release.

This parameter specifies the release with which Oracle must maintain compatibility. It allows you to take advantage of the maintenance improvements of a new release immediately in your production systems without testing the new functionality in your environment. Some features of the release may be restricted.

When using a standby database, this parameter must have the same value on both the primary and standby databases.

Note that as of Oracle 10^g, this parameter cannot be lowered once it has been set.

CONTROL_FILES

Table 3-8   CONTROL_FILES

Property	Description
Parameter type	String
Syntax	CONTROL_FILES = *filename* [, *filename*] … Note: The control filename can be an OMF name. This occurs when the control file is recreated using the CREATE CONTROLFILE REUSE statement.
Default value	OS-dependent
Modifiable	No
Range of values	1 to 8 filenames
Real Application Clusters	Multiple instances must have the same value

Every database has a control file that contains entries that describe the structure of the database (such as its name, the timestamp of its creation, and the names and locations of its datafiles and redo files). CONTROL_FILES specifies one or more names of control files, separated by commas.

Oracle Corporation recommends that you multiplex multiple control files on different devices or mirror the file at the OS level.

CORE_DUMP_DEST

Table 3-9   CORE_DUMP_DEST

Property	Description
Parameter type	String
Syntax	CORE_DUMP_DEST = *directory*
Default value	*ORACLE_HOME*/DBS
Modifiable	ALTER SYSTEM

CORE_DUMP_DEST is primarily a UNIX parameter and may not be supported on your platform. It specifies the directory where Oracle dumps core files.

DB_BLOCK_SIZE

Table 3-10 DB_BLOCK_SIZE

Property	Description
Parameter type	Integer
Default value	8192
Modifiable	Set at database create time, and completely unmodifiable thereafter
Range of values	2048 to 32768, but your OS may have a narrower range
Real Application Clusters	You must set this parameter for every instance, and multiple instances must have the same value

DB_BLOCK_SIZE specifies (in bytes) the size of Oracle database blocks. Typical values are 4096 and 8192. The value for DB_BLOCK_SIZE in effect at the time you create the database determines the size of the blocks. The value must remain set to its initial value.

For the Real Application Clusters feature, this parameter affects the maximum value of the FREELISTS storage parameter for tables and indexes. Oracle uses one database block for each free list group. Decision support system (DSS) and data warehouse database environments tend to benefit from larger block size values.

DB_CACHE_SIZE

Table 3-11 DB_CACHE_SIZE

Property	Description
Parameter type	Big integer
Syntax	DB_CACHE_SIZE = *integer* [K I M I G]
Default value	48M, rounded up to the nearest granule size
Modifiable	ALTER SYSTEM

DB_CACHE_SIZE specifies the size of the DEFAULT buffer pool for buffers with the primary block size (the block size defined by the DB_BLOCK_SIZE initialization parameter).

The value must be at least the size of one granule (smaller values are automatically rounded up to the granule size). A value of zero is illegal because zero is the size of the DEFAULT pool for the standard block size, which is the block size for the SYSTEM tablespace.

DB_CREATE_FILE_DEST

Table 3-12 DB_CREATE_FILE_DEST

Property	Description
Parameter type	String
Syntax	DB_CREATE_FILE_DEST = *directory*	*disk group*
Default value	No default
Modifiable	ALTER SESSION, ALTER SYSTEM

DB_CREATE_FILE_DEST specifies the default location for Oracle-managed datafiles. This location is also used as the default location for Oracle-managed control files and online redo logs if no DB_CREATE_ONLINE_LOG_DEST_*n* initialization parameters are specified.

If a filesystem directory is specified as the default location, then the directory must already exist; Oracle will not create it. The directory must have appropriate permissions that allow Oracle to create files in it. Oracle generates unique names for the files, and a file thus created is an Oracle-managed file.

DB_CREATE_ONLINE_LOG_DEST_n

Table 3-13   DB_CREATE_ONLINE_LOG_DEST_n

Property	Description
Parameter type	String
Syntax	DB_CREATE_ONLINE_LOG_DEST_{1|2|3|4|5} = *directory*	*disk group*
Default value	No default
Modifiable	ALTER SESSION, ALTER SYSTEM

DB_CREATE_ONLINE_LOG_DEST_n (where n = 1, 2, 3, ... 5) specifies the default location for Oracle-managed control files and online redo logs. If more than one DB_CREATE_ONLINE_LOG_DEST_n parameter is specified, then the control file or online redo log is multiplexed across the locations of the other DB_CREATE_ONLINE_LOG_DEST_n parameters. One member of each online redo log is created in each location, and one control file is created in each location.

Specifying at least two parameters provides greater fault tolerance for the control files and online redo logs if one of the locations should fail.

If a filesystem directory is specified as the default location, then the directory must already exist; Oracle does not create it. The directory must have appropriate permissions that allow Oracle to create files in it. Oracle generates unique names for the files, and a file thus created is an Oracle-managed file.

DB_DOMAIN

Table 3-14 DB_DOMAIN

Property	Description
Parameter type	String
Syntax	DB_DOMAIN = *domain name*
Default value	No default
Modifiable	No
Range of values	Any legal string of name components, separated by periods and up to 128 characters long (including the periods); this value cannot be NULL
Real Application Clusters	You must set this parameter for every instance, and multiple instances must have the same value

In a distributed database system, DB_DOMAIN specifies the logical location of the database within the network structure. You should set this parameter if this database is or ever will be part of a distributed system. The value consists of the extension components of a global database name, including valid identifiers separated by periods. Oracle Corporation recommends that you specify DB_DOMAIN as a unique string for all databases in a domain.

This parameter allows one department to create a database without worrying that it might have the same name as a database created by another department. If one sales department's DB_DOMAIN is JAPAN.ACME.COM, then its SALES database (SALES.JAPAN.ACME.COM) is uniquely distinguished from another database with DB_NAME = SALES, but with DB_DOMAIN = US.ACME.COM.

If you omit the domains from the name of a database link, Oracle expands the name by qualifying the database with the domain of your local database as it currently exists in the data dictionary, and then stores the link name in the data dictionary. The characters valid in a database domain name are: alphanumeric characters, underscore (_), and pound sign (#).

DB_NAME

Table 3-15 DB_NAME

Property	Description
Parameter type	String
Syntax	DB_NAME = *database name*
Default value	No default
Modifiable	No
Range of values	Any legal name string, up to 8 characters long; this value cannot be NULL
Real Application Clusters	You must set this parameter for every instance, and multiple instances must have the same value, or the same value must be specified in the STARTUP OPEN command or the ALTER DATABASE MOUNT statement

DB_NAME specifies a database identifier of up to eight characters. This parameter must be specified and must correspond to the name specified in the CREATE DATABASE statement.

If you have multiple databases, the value of this parameter should match the Oracle instance identifier of each one to avoid confusion with other databases running on the system. The value of DB_NAME should be the same in both the standby and production initialization parameter files.

The database name specified in either the STARTUP command or the ALTER DATABASE ... MOUNT statement for each instance of the cluster database must correspond to the DB_NAME initialization parameter setting.

The following characters are valid in a database name: alphanumeric characters, underscore (_), pound sign (#), and dollar sign ($). No other characters are valid. Oracle removes double quotation marks before processing the database name; therefore, you cannot use double quotation marks to embed other characters in the name. The database name is case-insensitive.

DB_RECOVERY_FILE_DEST

Table 3-16 DB_RECOVERY_FILE_DEST

Property	Description
Parameter type	String
Syntax	DB_CREATE_FILE_DEST = *directory*	*disk group*
Default value	No default
Modifiable	ALTER SYSTEM … SID=*
Real Application Clusters	You must set this parameter for every instance, and multiple instances must have the same value

DB_RECOVERY_FILE_DEST specifies the default location for the recovery area. The recovery area contains multiplexed copies of current control files and online redo logs, as well as archived redo logs, flashback logs, and RMAN backups.

Specifying this parameter without also specifying the DB_RECOVERY_FILE_DEST_SIZE initialization parameter is not allowed.

DB_RECOVERY_FILE_DEST_SIZE

Table 3-17 DB_RECOVERY_FILE_DEST_SIZE

Property	Description
Parameter type	Big integer
Syntax	DB_CREATE_FILE_DEST_SIZE = *integer* [K| M | G]
Default value	0
Modifiable	ALTER SYSTEM ... SID=*
Real Application Clusters	You must set this parameter for every instance, and multiple instances must have the same value

DB_RECOVERY_FILE_DEST_SIZE specifies (in bytes) the hard limit on the total space to be used by target database recovery files created in the recovery area location.

Disabling this parameter without also disabling DB_RECOVERY_FILE_DEST will produce an error.

INSTANCE_NUMBER

Table 3-18 INSTANCE_NUMBER

Property	Description
Parameter type	Integer
Syntax	INSTANCE_NUMBER = *integer*
Default value	Lowest available number based on instance startup order and INSTANCE_NUMBER value of other instances; if not configured for Real Application Clusters, then 0
Modifiable	No
Range of values	1 to maximum number of instances specified when the database was created
Real Application Clusters	You must set this parameter for every instance, and multiple instances must have different values

INSTANCE_NUMBER is a Real Application Clusters parameter that can be specified in either parallel or exclusive mode. It specifies a unique number that maps the instance to one free list group for each database object created with storage parameter FREELIST GROUPS.

The INSTANCE parameter of the ALTER TABLE ... ALLOCATE EXTENT statement assigns an extent to a particular free list group. If you set INSTANCE_NUMBER to the value specified for the INSTANCE parameter, the instance uses that extent for inserts and for updates that expand rows.

The practical maximum value of this parameter is the maximum number of instances specified in the CREATE DATABASE statement. The absolute maximum is OS-dependent.

JAVA_POOL_SIZE

Table 3-19 JAVA_POOL_SIZE

Property	Description
Parameter type	Big integer
Syntax	JAVA_POOL_SIZE = *integer* [K I M I G]
Default value	24M, rounded up to the nearest granule size
Modifiable	ALTER SYSTEM
Range of values	Minimum of 0, with values greater than zero being rounded up to the nearest granule size; maximum is OS-dependent

JAVA_POOL_SIZE specifies (in bytes) the size of the Java pool from which the Java memory manager allocates most Java states during runtime execution. This memory includes the shared in-memory representation of Java method and class definitions, as well as the Java objects that are migrated to the Java session space at the end-of-call.

Basic Initialization (init.ora) Parameters

JOB_QUEUE_PROCESSES

Table 3-20 JOB_QUEUE_PROCESSES

Property	Description
Parameter type	Integer
Syntax	JOB_QUEUE_PROCESSES = *integer*
Default value	0
Modifiable	ALTER SYSTEM
Range of values	0 to 1000
Real Application Clusters	Multiple instances can have different values

JOB_QUEUE_PROCESSES specifies the maximum number of processes that can be created for job execution. It specifies the number of job queue processes per instance (J000, ... J999). Replication uses job queues for data refreshes. Advanced queuing uses job queues for message propagation. You can create user job requests through the DBMS_JOB package.

Some job queue requests are created automatically. An example is refresh support for materialized views. To have your materialized views updated automatically, you must set JOB_QUEUE_PROCESSES to a value of one or higher.

LARGE_POOL_SIZE

Table 3-21 LARGE_POOL_SIZE

Property	Description
Parameter type	Big integer
Syntax	LARGE_POOL_SIZE = *integer* [K l M l G]
Default value	0 if and only if the pool is not required by parallel execution and DBWR_IO_SLAVES is not set
Modifiable	ALTER SYSTEM
Range of values	300K to at least 2G; actual maximum is OS-specific

LARGE_POOL_SIZE specifies (in bytes) the size of the large pool allocation heap. The large pool allocation heap is used in shared server systems for session memory, by parallel execution for message buffers, and by backup processes for disk input/output (I/O) buffers. Parallel execution allocates buffers out of the large pool only when PARALLEL_AUTOMATIC_TUNING is set to TRUE.

You can specify the value of this parameter using a number, optionally followed by K or M to specify kilobytes or megabytes, respectively. If you do not specify K or M, then the number is taken as bytes.

LOG_ARCHIVE_DEST_n

Table 3-22   LOG_ARCHIVE_DEST_n

Property	Description
Parameter type	String
Syntax	LOG_ARCHIVE_DEST_[1|2|3|4|5|6|7|8|9|10] =
	{ *null string*	
	{ LOCATION=*path_name*	SERVICE=*service_name* }
	[{ MANDATORY	OPTIONAL }]
	[REOPEN[=*seconds*]	NOREOPEN]
	[DELAY[=*minutes*]	NODELAY]
	[REGISTER[=*template*]	NOREGISTER]
	[TEMPLATE[=*template*]	NOTEMPLATE]
	[ALTERNATE[=*destination*]	NOALTERNATE]
	[DEPENDENCY[=*destination*]	NODEPENDENCY]
	[MAX_FAILURE[=*count*]	NOMAX_FAILURE]
	[QUOTA_SIZE[=*blocks*]	NOQUOTA_SIZE]
	[QUOTA_USED[=*blocks*]	NOQUOTA_USED]
	[ARCH	LGWR]
	[SYNC[=PARALLEL	NOPARALLEL]	

Table 3-22 LOG_ARCHIVE_DEST_n (continued)

Property	Description
	ASYNC[=*blocks*]] [AFFIRM | NOAFFIRM] [NET_TIMEOUT=*seconds* | NONET_TIMEOUT] [VALID_FOR=(*redo_log_type, database_role*)] [DB_UNIQUE_NAME | NODB_UNIQUE_NAME] [VERIFY | NOVERIFY] }
Default value	No default
Modifiable	ALTER SESSION, ALTER SYSTEM

The LOG_ARCHIVE_DEST_*n* parameters (where *n* = 1, 2, 3, ... 10) define up to 10 archive log destinations. The parameter integer suffix is defined as the handle displayed by the V$ARCHIVE_DEST dynamic performance view.

Values

SERVICE—Specifies a standby destination. Oracle Net (inter-process communication [IPC] or Transmission Control Protocol [TCP]) transmits the archive log. A standby instance must be associated with the destination. The value represented by *tnsnames_service* corresponds to an appropriate service name in tnsnames.ora.

LOCATION—Specifies a local filesystem destination. You must specify this parameter for at least one destination.

MANDATORY—Specifies that archiving to the destination must succeed before the redo log file can be made available for reuse.

OPTIONAL—Specifies that successful archiving to the destination is not required before the redo log file can be made available for reuse. If the "must succeed count" set with LOG_ARCHIVE_MIN_SUCCEED_DEST is met, the redo log file is marked for reuse. This is the default.

REOPEN—Specifies the minimum number of seconds before the archiver process (ARC*n*, foreground, or log writer process) should try again to access a previously failed destination. Future attempts are made when the next redo log file is archived. If a destination is MANDATORY, then Oracle Corporation recommends that you specify a REOPEN time that reduces the possibility of primary database shutdown due to lack of available online redo log files. If you do not specify seconds, the default value is 300 seconds.

LOG_ARCHIVE_DEST_STATE_n

Table 3-23 LOG_ARCHIVE_DEST_STATE_n

Property	Description
Parameter type	String
Syntax	LOG_ARCHIVE_DEST_STATE_[1|2|3|4|5|6|7|8|9|10] = { ALTERNATE	RESET	DEFER	ENABLE }
Default value	ENABLE
Modifiable	ALTER SESSION, ALTER SYSTEM

The LOG_ARCHIVE_DEST_STATE_n parameters (where n = 1, 2, 3, ... 10) specify the availability state of the corresponding destination. The parameter suffix (1 through 10) specifies one of the ten corresponding LOG_ARCHIVE_DEST_n destination parameters.

Values

ENABLED—Specifies that a valid log archive destination can be used for a subsequent archiving operation (automatic or manual). This is the default.

DEFER—Specifies that valid destination information and attributes are preserved, but the destination is excluded from archiving operations until re-enabled.

ALTERNATE—Specifies that a log archive destination is not enabled, but will become enabled if communications to another destination fail. The LOG_ARCHIVE_DEST_STATE_n parameters have no effect on the ENABLE state of the LOG_ARCHIVE_DEST and LOG_ARCHIVE_DUPLEX_DEST parameters.

The V$ARCHIVE_DEST dynamic performance view shows values in use for the current session. The DEST_ID column of that view corresponds to the archive destination suffix "n".

NLS_LANGUAGE

Table 3-24 NLS_LANGUAGE

Property	Description
Parameter type	String
Syntax	NLS_LANGUAGE = *language*
Default value	OS-dependent; derived from the NLS_LANG environment variable
Modifiable	ALTER SESSION
Range of values	Any valid language name

NLS_LANGUAGE specifies the default language of the database. This language is used for messages, day and month names, symbols for AD and BC, a.m. and p.m., and the default sorting mechanism. This parameter also determines the default values of the parameters NLS_DATE_LANGUAGE and NLS_SORT.

NLS_TERRITORY

Table 3-25 NLS_TERRITORY

Property	Description
Parameter type	String
Syntax	NLS_TERRITORY = *territory*
Default value	OS-dependent
Modifiable	ALTER SESSION
Range of values	Any valid territory name

NLS_TERRITORY specifies the name of the territory whose conventions are to be followed for day and week numbering. This parameter also establishes the default date format, the default decimal character and group separator, and the default International Organization for Standardization (ISO) and local currency symbols.

OPEN_CURSORS

Table 3-26 OPEN_CURSORS

Property	Description
Parameter type	Integer
Syntax	OPEN_CURSORS = *integer*
Default value	50
Modifiable	ALTER SYSTEM
Range of values	1 to 4294967295 ($2^{32} - 1$)

OPEN_CURSORS specifies the maximum number of open cursors (handles to private SQL areas) a session can have at once. You can use this parameter to prevent a session from opening an excessive number of cursors. This parameter also constrains the size of the PL/SQL cursor cache which PL/SQL uses to avoid having to reparse as statements are re-executed by a user.

It is important to set the value of OPEN_CURSORS high enough to keep your application from running out of open cursors. The number will vary from one application to another. Assuming that a session does not open the number of cursors specified by OPEN_CURSORS, there is no added overhead to setting this value higher than actually needed.

PGA_AGGREGATE_TARGET

Table 3-27   PGA_AGGREGATE_TARGET

Property	Description
Parameter type	Big integer
Syntax	PGA_AGGREGATE_TARGET = *integer* [K I M I G]
Default value	10M or 20% of the size of the SGA, whichever is greater
Modifiable	ALTER SYSTEM
Range of values	Minimum: 10M Maximum: 4096G – 1

PGA_AGGREGATE_TARGET specifies the target aggregate Program Global Area (PGA) memory available to all server processes attached to the instance. You must set this parameter to enable the automatic sizing of SQL working areas used by memory-intensive SQL operators such as sort, group-by, hash-join, bitmap merge, and bitmap create.

Oracle uses this parameter as a target for PGA memory. Use this parameter to determine the optimal size of each work area allocated in AUTO mode (in other words, when WORKAREA_SIZE_POLICY is set to AUTO).

Oracle attempts to keep the amount of private memory below the target specified by this parameter by adapting the size of the work areas to private memory. When increasing the value of this parameter, you indirectly increase the memory allotted to work areas. Consequently, more memory-intensive operations are able to run fully in memory and less will work their way over to disk.

When setting this parameter, you should examine the total memory on your system that is available to the Oracle instance and subtract the SGA. You can assign the remaining memory to PGA_AGGREGATE_TARGET.

PROCESSES

Table 3-28   PROCESSES

Property	Description
Parameter type	Integer
Syntax	PROCESSES = *integer*
Default value	Derived from PARALLEL_MAX_SERVERS
Modifiable	No
Range of values	6 to OS-dependent
Real Application Clusters	Multiple instances can have different values

The PROCESSES parameter specifies the maximum number of OS user processes that can simultaneously connect to Oracle. Its value should allow for all background processes such as locks, job queue processes, and parallel execution processes.

The default values of the SESSIONS and TRANSACTIONS parameters are derived from this parameter. Therefore, if you change the value of PROCESSES, you should evaluate whether to adjust the values of those derived parameters.

REMOTE_LISTENER

Table 3-29 REMOTE_LISTENER

Property	Description
Parameter type	String
Syntax	REMOTE_LISTENER = *network_name*
Default value	No default
Modifiable	ALTER SYSTEM

REMOTE_LISTENER specifies a network name that resolves to an address or address list of Oracle Net remote listeners (that is, listeners that are not running on the same machine as this instance). The address or address list is specified in the TNSNAMES.ORA file or other address repository as configured for your system.

REMOTE_LOGIN_PASSWORDFILE

Table 3-30 REMOTE_LOGIN_PASSWORDFILE

Property	Description
Parameter type	String
Syntax	REMOTE_LOGIN_PASSWORDFILE = [NONE	SHARED	EXCLUSIVE]
Default value	NONE
Modifiable	No
Real Application Clusters	Multiple instances must have the same value

REMOTE_LOGIN_PASSWORDFILE specifies whether Oracle checks for a password file and how many databases can use the password file.

Values

NONE—Oracle ignores any password file. Therefore, privileged users must be authenticated by the OS.

SHARED—More than one database can use a password file. However, the only user recognized by the password file is SYS.

EXCLUSIVE—The password file can be used by only one database and the password file can contain names other than SYS.

ROLLBACK_SEGMENTS

Table 3-31 ROLLBACK_SEGMENTS

Property	Description
Parameter type	String
Syntax	ROLLBACK_SEGMENTS = (*segment_name* [, *segment_name*] …)
Default value	The instance uses public rollback segments by default if you do not specify this parameter
Modifiable	No
Range of values	Any rollback segment names listed in DBA_ROLLBACK_SEGS, except SYSTEM
Real Application Clusters	Multiple instance must have different values

ROLLBACK_SEGMENTS allocates one or more rollback segments by name to this instance. If you set this parameter, the instance acquires all of the rollback segments named in this parameter, even if the number of rollback segments exceeds the minimum number required by the instance (calculated as TRANSACTIONS / TRANSACTIONS_PER_ROLLBACK_SEGMENT).

You cannot change the value of this parameter dynamically, but you can change its value and then restart the instance. Although this parameter usually specifies private rollback segments, it can also specify public rollback segments if they are not already in use.

To find the name, segment ID number, and status of each rollback segment in the database, query the data dictionary view DBA_ROLLBACK_SEGS. When UNDO_MANAGEMENT is set to AUTO, ROLLBACK_SEGMENTS is ignored.

SESSIONS

Table 3-32 SESSIONS

Property	Description
Parameter type	Integer
Syntax	SESSIONS = *integer*
Default value	Derived: (1.1 * PROCESSES) + 5
Modifiable	No
Range of values	1 to 2^{31}

SESSIONS specifies the maximum number of sessions that can be created in the system. Because every login requires a session, this parameter effectively determines the maximum number of concurrent users in the system. You should always set this parameter explicitly to a value equivalent to your estimate of the maximum number of concurrent users, plus the number of background processes, plus approximately 10% for recursive sessions.

Oracle uses the default value of this parameter as its minimum. Values between 1 and the default do not trigger errors, but Oracle ignores them and uses the default instead.

The default values of the ENQUEUE_RESOURCES and TRANSACTIONS parameters are derived from SESSIONS. Therefore, if you increase the value of SESSIONS, you should consider whether to adjust the values of ENQUEUE_RESOURCES and TRANSACTIONS as well.

In a shared server environment, the value of PROCESSES can be quite small. Therefore, Oracle Corporation recommends that you adjust the value of SESSIONS to approximately 1.1 * total number of connections.

SGA_TARGET

Table 3-33   SGA_TARGET

Property	Description
Parameter type	Big integer
Syntax	SGA_TARGET = *integer* [K	M	G]
Default value	0 (SGA auto-tuning is disabled, by default)
Modifiable	ALTER SYSTEM
Range of values	64 to OS-dependent

SGA_TARGET specifies the total size of all SGA components. If SGA_TARGET is specified, then the following memory pools are automatically sized:

- Buffer cache (DB_CACHE_SIZE)
- Shared pool (SHARED_POOL_SIZE)
- Large pool (LARGE_POOL_SIZE)
- Java pool (JAVA_POOL_SIZE)

SHARED_POOL_SIZE

Table 3-34 SHARED_POOL_SIZE

Property	Description
Parameter type	Big integer
Syntax	SHARED_POOL_SIZE = *integer* [K | M | G]
Default value	32-bit: 8M 64-bit: 64M All settings are rounded up to the nearest granule size
Modifiable	ALTER SYSTEM
Range of values	Minimum: the granule size Maximum: OS-dependent

SHARED_POOL_SIZE specifies (in bytes) the size of the shared pool. The shared pool contains shared cursors, stored procedures, control structures, and other structures. If you set PARALLEL_AUTOMATIC_TUNING to FALSE, then Oracle also allocates parallel execution message buffers from the shared pool. Larger values improve performance in multi-user systems. Smaller values use less memory.

You can monitor utilization of the shared pool by querying the view V$SGASTAT.

SHARED_SERVERS

Table 3-35 SHARED_SERVERS

Property	Description
Parameter type	Integer
Syntax	SHARED_SERVERS = *integer*
Default value	0, meaning that shared server usage is disabled
Modifiable	ALTER SYSTEM
Range of values	The value of this parameter should be less than MAX_SHARED_SERVERS; if greater than or equal to MAX_SHARED_SERVERS, the number of servers will not be self-tuned, but will remain constant, as specified by this parameter

SHARED_SERVERS specifies the number of server processes to create when an instance is started. If system load decreases, then this minimum number of servers is maintained. Therefore, you should take care not to set SHARED_SERVERS too high at system startup.

STAR_TRANSFORMATION_ENABLED

Table 3-36 STAR_TRANSFORMATION_ENABLED

Property	Description
Parameter type	String
Syntax	STAR_TRANSFORMATION_ENABLED = [TEMP_DISABLE I TRUE I FALSE]
Default value	FALSE
Modifiable	ALTER SESSION, ALTER SYSTEM

STAR_TRANSFORMATION_ENABLED determines whether a cost-based query transformation will be applied to star queries.

Values

TRUE—The optimizer will consider performing a cost-based query transformation on the star query.

FALSE—The transformation will not be applied.

TEMP_DISABLE—The optimizer will consider performing a cost-based query transformation on the star query, but will not use temporary tables in the star transformation.

UNDO_MANAGEMENT

Table 3-37   UNDO_MANAGEMENT

Property	Description
Parameter type	String
Syntax	UNDO_MANAGEMENT = [MANUAL	AUTO]
Default value	MANUAL
Modifiable	No
Real Application Clusters	Multiple instances must have the same value

UNDO_MANAGEMENT specifies which undo space management mode the system should use. When set to AUTO, the instance starts in automatic undo management mode. In manual undo management mode, undo space is allocated externally as rollback segments.

UNDO_TABLESPACE

Table 3-38   UNDO_TABLESPACE

Property	Description
Parameter type	String
Syntax	UNDO_TABLESPACE = *tablespace_name*
Default value	The first available undo tablespace in the database
Modifiable	ALTER SYSTEM
Range of values	Legal name of an existing undo tablespace
Real Application Clusters	Multiple instances can have different values

UNDO_TABLESPACE specifies the undo tablespace to be used when an instance starts up. If this parameter is specified when the instance is in manual undo management mode, an error will occur and startup will fail.

If the UNDO_TABLESPACE parameter is omitted, the first available undo tablespace in the database is chosen. If no undo tablespace is available, the instance will start without an undo tablespace. In such cases, user transactions will be executed using the SYSTEM rollback segment. You should avoid running in this mode under normal circumstances.

You can replace an undo tablespace with another undo tablespace while the instance is running.

USER_DUMP_DEST

Table 3-39   USER_DUMP_DEST

Property	Description
Parameter type	String
Syntax	USER_DUMP_DEST = [*pathname* | *directory*]
Default value	OS-dependent
Modifiable	ALTER SYSTEM
Range of values	Any valid local path, directory, or disk

USER_DUMP_DEST specifies the pathname for a directory where the server will write debugging trace files on behalf of a user process.

ORADIM COMMAND LINE PARAMETERS

The ORADIM tool supports the command line parameters described in Table 3-40. Use "oradim -help" for more syntax definition.

Table 3-40 ORADIM Command Line Parameters

Parameter	Purpose	Additional Comments
-NEW	Tells ORADIM to create a new database service.	Only NEW, EDIT, DELETE, STARTUP, or SHUTDOWN can be specified.
-EDIT	Tells ORADIM to edit an existing service.	Only NEW, EDIT, DELETE, STARTUP, or SHUTDOWN can be specified.
-DELETE	Tells ORADIM to delete an existing service.	Only NEW, EDIT, DELETE, STARTUP, or SHUTDOWN can be specified.
-STARTUP	Tells ORADIM to start an existing service.	Only NEW, EDIT, DELETE, STARTUP, or SHUTDOWN can be specified.

Table 3-40   ORADIM Command Line Parameters (continued)

Parameter	Purpose	Additional Comments
-SHUTDOWN	Tells ORADIM to stop an existing service.	Only NEW, EDIT, DELETE, STARTUP, or SHUTDOWN can be specified.
-SID <database SID>	Specifies the database SID for which this service is to be configured.	This argument is mandatory in every version of the command.
-SRVC <service name>	Tells ORADIM what to name the service.	This parameter is optional.
-OSMSID <ASM SID>	Identifies this as an ASM instance, and tells ORADIM the associated SID.	Mutually exclusive with -SID.
-OSMSRVC <service name>	Tells ORADIM what to name the ASM service.	This parameter is optional and is mutually exclusive with -SRVC.
-SYSPWD <password> (10^g) -INITPWD <password> (9*i*) -USRPWD <password> (9*i*)	Provides ORADIM with the SYSDBA password.	If OS authentication is enabled, this parameter is optional.

Table 3-40 ORADIM Command Line Parameters (continued)

Parameter	Purpose	Additional Comments
-STARTMODE [a l m]	Defines the startup mode for the service.	a = automatic m = manual
-SRVCSTART [system l demand]	Defines when the database service should start.	"system" means to start at boot time; "demand" means to start the first time the database is accessed.
-PFILE <filename>	Designates which init.ora file to use when starting the database.	Mutually exclusive with -SPFILE.
-SPFILE	Tells ORADIM to configure the service to expect a server parameter file at startup.	SPFILE must be in the default location, which is currently ORACLE_HOME\database.
-SHUTMODE [n l i l a]	Defines what type of shutdown to issue when the service is stopped.	n = normal i = immediate a = abort
-TIMEOUT <seconds>	Specifies the number of seconds to wait for database shutdown before stopping the service.	

Table 3-40 ORADIM Command Line Parameters (continued)

Parameter	Purpose	Additional Comments
-RUNAS <OS user>/<OS password>	Causes the database to be started with a specific user as the process owner.	
-NEWSID <database SID>	Tells ORADIM that the database associated with an existing service has been renamed.	Used only with the EDIT command.
-STARTTYPE [srvc | srvc,inst]	Defines whether just the service should be started, or both the service and the instance.	
-SHUTTYPE [inst | srvc,inst]	Defines whether just the instance should be shut down, or both the instance and the service.	
-? -h -help	Tells ORADIM to print its help screen and exit.	

Chapter Four

Day-to-Day Administration

USE WHAT'S ALREADY THERE

After the software has been installed and the database created, the DBA finally reaches the real meat of the job. For the experienced DBA, there's a very real tendency to keep using the tools they've always used, even if they were originally created for use with Oracle 7. The fledgling DBA can run into similar problems, since it's difficult to discover all of the different automation opportunities included with Oracle, while simultaneously dealing with demands from users, developers, and management. In spite of these challenges, or even because of them, it's vitally important to automate as much as possible. It's equally important to avoid recreating a capability that's already available. The two most recent versions of Oracle have added an almost unbelievable wealth of options for the over-worked DBA to automate his or her way to a quieter pager.

TEST EVERYTHING FIRST

With the multitude of new capabilities in recent versions, there's a temptation to implement everything that the documentation says will help improve operations or performance. It's important to resist that temptation, just enough to allow time for the testing of each and every new feature prior to implementation. Some of the new features will help in all situations, some will help in all but a few situations, and a few might create problems in certain circumstances. Testing prior to implementation is absolutely vital.

FILE AND TABLESPACE MANAGEMENT

Starting in Oracle 8i, but especially in Oracle 9i and Oracle 10^g, Oracle provides a number of tablespace and file management options that the DBA can take advantage of to automate space management. While not all options are ideally suited for all environments, the judicious use of the ones that are appropriate, especially in Oracle 10^g, can significantly reduce the amount of time and attention the DBA needs to spend on space management.

Automatic Undo Management

Prior to Oracle 9*i*, a DBA had to manage rollback tablespaces and rollback segments manually. Failure to allocate enough segments, or to allocate enough space for those segments, would invariably leads to complaints from users about the dreaded "ORA-01555: snapshot too old" error during long transactions. Since the advent of 9*i*, that worry can, and should, largely be eliminated.

In version 9.0, three new initialization parameters were added: UNDO_MANAGEMENT, UNDO_RETENTION, and UNDO_TABLESPACE. To activate automatic undo management, you should first make sure that at least one undo tablespace exists. If none exist, one should be created. After that, set the UNDO_MANAGEMENT parameter to AUTO, either via the pfile or spfile, or dynamically with ALTER SYSTEM. If the UNDO_TABLESPACE parameter is not set, Oracle will automatically use the first available undo tablespace. If the UNDO_RETENTION parameter is not set, or is set to 0 (zero), Oracle will automatically tune for maximum retention of undo information based on the space available in the target undo tablespace, with the caveat that this automatic tuning mechanism will never tune for less than 15 minutes of retention. Setting the UNDO_RETENTION PARAMETER to a non-zero value forces a specific undo retention time (in minutes) and disables automatic retention tuning.

Locally Managed Tablespaces

Introduced in Oracle 8*i*, locally managed tablespaces represent a radical change in how Oracle tracks space allocation inside tablespaces. Prior to Oracle 8*i*, all tablespaces were "dictionary-managed," meaning that all extent allocation was tracked by tables in the database's SYSTEM tablespace. A locally managed tablespace manages its own space, using a bitmap stored in each datafile. Each bit in the bitmap represents one or more blocks in the datafile. As extents are allocated and deallocated, bits in the bitmap are set or cleared. The bitmap mechanism means that there is no need to coalesce free space in a locally managed tablespace. Also, more efficient extent tracking means that the number of extents in a segment has essentially no impact on performance, thus freeing the DBA from worrying about table reorganization.

Since space management operations no longer involve the SYSTEM tablespace, no recursive space management is required, fewer object locks are needed, and no rollback space is required. This can result in a noticeable performance improvement in very dynamic database environments.

In Oracle 8*i* and 9*i* release 1, the SYSTEM tablespace could not be locally managed. Starting with 9*i* release 2, that restriction is removed. If the SYSTEM tablespace is set to locally managed, then all other tablespaces in the database must use the same setting. After 9*i* release 2, there are very few reasons to continue using dictionary-managed tablespaces.

When creating a locally managed tablespace, or LMT, you must choose between allowing Oracle to automatically manage the size of extents in the tablespace or forcing all extents to be the same size. To create a tablespace in which Oracle manages the extent size, use the following command:

```
CREATE TABLESPACE autotbsp
    EXTENT MANAGEMENT LOCAL AUTOALLOCATE;
```

The AUTOALLOCATE setting tells Oracle to automatically determine the size of each extent at the time it is allocated. The exact algorithm is unpublished, but no extent smaller than 64k will be allocated, and as a segment requests new extents, the size of each extent will grow. By using progressively larger extents in a segment, Oracle can minimize—somewhat—the number of extents in each segment. Unfortunately, these variable extent sizes can lead to "bubble" fragmentation in a tablespace, in which blocks of unallocated space are too small to hold new extents, thus causing segment extensions to fail, even when there's still room left in the tablespace. Because of this, auto-allocated tablespaces are best left for fairly static data.

Using a single, uniform extent size in every tablespace has long been a common DBA strategy. In typical Oracle fashion, they have adopted and adapted that strategy to their product. Creating a tablespace that automatically uses this strategy is done with the following command:

```
CREATE TABLESPACE uniformtbsp EXTENT MANAGEMENT LOCAL
    UNIFORM SIZE 1M;
```

The UNIFORM setting tells Oracle that all extents in this tablespace should be forced to the same size. The SIZE 1M phrase defines the forced size as one megabyte, which is also the default.

In both auto-allocate and uniform LMTs, an object's INITIAL, NEXT, and MINEXTENT settings will be taken into account during object creation and extension, but will not be followed exactly. In the previous example, a table created with INITIAL 512K and MINEXTENTS 4 would actually start with four megabytes of initial storage, since all extents in the tablespace must be 1M. Similarly, a table created with INITIAL 2M and MINEXTENTS 1 would be created with two extents of one megabyte each. An auto-allocate tablespace takes similar account of an object's storage settings, but the results are less predictable.

When sizing LMT datafiles, bear in mind that some space in each file will be used to store the bitmap. In both auto-allocate and uniform tablespace datafiles, this will result in 64K of "invisible" space. For uniform tablespaces, datafiles should be sized such that they are an even multiple of their extent size, plus 64K. If the extra 64K is not allocated, one entire extent will be "invisible," since not enough space will be left after the 64K bitmap is subtracted to allocate a full extent.

Starting with Oracle 8.1.6, you can migrate dictionary-managed tablespaces to locally managed using the MIGRATE_TO_LOCAL procedure in the DBMS_SPACE_ADMIN PL/SQL package. Should any problems arise, the tablespace can be migrated back to dictionary-managed using the MIGRATE_FROM_LOCAL procedure of the same package. The only restrictions to this migration are that the SYSTEM tablespace can't be migrated, nor can temporary or offline tablespaces.

Automatic Segment Space Management

Initially delivered in Oracle *9i* release 1, automatic segment space management, or ASSM, is another feature that has the potential of relieving the DBA of some management headaches while simultaneously improving performance. ASSM can only be used in permanent LMTs. In a non-ASSM tablespace, available space within an object is tracked with freelists. When not properly tuned, freelists (and freelist groups) can lead to performance bottlenecks in Real Application Clusters(RAC) or high-throughput environments. Creating an object in an ASSM tablespace eliminates those concerns and should outperform all but the most painstakingly tuned non-ASSM objects. Furthermore, using ASSM completely removes the need for calculating or tuning not only freelists and freelist groups, but also "pctused" settings. An ASSM tablespace can be created with the following command:

```
CREATE TABLESPACE assm_tbsp
EXTENT MANAGEMENT LOCAL UNIFORM SIZE 2M
SEGMENT SPACE MANAGEMENT AUTO;
```

 Note: ASSM is not available on dictionary-managed tablespaces. Tables with large object (LOB) columns can't be created in tablespaces using ASSM in releases of Oracle prior to Oracle *9i* release 2.

Given its advantages, ASSM should almost always be the preferred choice on Oracle *9i* release 2 or later versions of Oracle.

Oracle-Managed Files

The OMF feature was introduced in Oracle 9*i* and can, under certain circumstances, be used very effectively. In essence, OMF allows Oracle to manage filenames and locations on its own, rather than requiring explicit instructions from the DBA. Dat files, control files, and even redo logs are named automatically when created. When tablespaces are dropped, any files created with OMF are automatically deleted.

OMF is activated by setting the DB_CREATE_FILE_DEST parameter to point to a valid filesystem directory. Optionally, you can also set the DB_CREATE_ONLINE_LOG_DEST_*n* parameters, where *n* is an integer between one and five. Once the DB_CREATE_FILE_DEST parameter is set, Oracle will automatically generate a name for new files, and will place those files in the designated directory. The DB_CREATE_ONLINE_LOG_DEST_*n* parameter is used to tell Oracle that it should multiplex online redo logs and control files into as many as five additional locations. The following is an example of creating a tablespace with OMF. The OMF-related parameters can be changed at any time, either by editing the pfile or spfile or by using the ALTER SYSTEM command. After changing one of these parameters, any new files will be created in the new destination, but old files will not be relocated.

```
CREATE TABLESPACE omf_tbsp
  DATAFILE SIZE 100M AUTOEXTEND ON NEXT 50M MAXSIZE UNLIMITED;
```

As shown in Chapter 3, all datafiles can be created using OMF, provided the appropriate parameters are set prior to issuing the CREATE DATABASE command.

Enabling OMF does not disable any other database functionality, meaning that manually named and managed files can still be used whenever desired. You can even combine OMF and non-OMF files in the same tablespace. The only restriction is that the manually named files will not be automatically deleted if the tablespace is dropped, unless the INCLUDING CONTENTS AND DATAFILES clause is appended to the DROP TABLESPACE command.

Since only a single destination can be specified for datafiles at any given time, OMF is not well-suited for all databases. If you're using a logical volume manager (LVM) and all of your datafiles exist in a single filesystem, then you may want to consider using OMF to simplify file management. Databases built on traditional filesystems, using multiple mount points or drive letters, will not lend themselves to OMF quite so readily. Another excellent use for OMF is for developmental databases, where ease of management is paramount.

Bigfile Tablespaces

Starting with Oracle10g, tablespaces can be created with the BIGFILE option, which specifies that the tablespace will consist of only a single datafile, which can be up to 8 exabytes (8 million terabytes) in size. Using a single large file can drastically simplify storage management in very large databases. Obviously, these extremely large files are only suitable for use on disk arrays. Generally, bigfile tablespaces must be locally managed and must use ASSM.

All normal tablespace **CREATE** and **ALTER** operations work with bigfile tablespaces, with the obvious exception of adding a datafile. Since they must consist only of a single datafile, attempting to add another file to a bigfile tablespace will result in an error. When specifying file or file extension sizes for bigfiles, you can specify sizes in gigabytes or terabytes by using the "G" and "T" abbreviations, respectively. For example:

```
CREATE BIGFILE TABLESPACE big_tbs
DATAFILE SIZE 2T AUTOEXTEND ON NEXT 500G MAXSIZE 200T
EXTENT MANAGEMENT LOCAL UNIFORM SIZE 50G
SEGMENT SPACE MANAGEMENT AUTO;
```

At database create time, you can indicate that the database should default to creating bigfile tablespaces rather than normal (smallfile) ones. To do this, include the SET DEFAULT BIGFILE TABLESPACE clause in the CREATE DATABASE statement as follows:

```
CREATE DATABASE bigdb
SET DEFAULT BIGFILE TABLESPACE
UNDO TABLESPACE undotbs
DEFAULT TEMPORARY TABLESPACE temp01;
```

If you set bigfile tablespaces as the default at database creation time, you can still create smallfile tablespaces by simply using the CREATE SMALLFILE TABLESPACE command.

You can also, at database create time, designate the undo and/or temporary tablespaces as bigfile tablespaces by adding the BIGFILE qualifier to the appropriate phrase of the CREATE DATABASE command; for instance:

```
CREATE DATABASE bigdb2
BIGFILE UNDO TABLESPACE undotbs DATAFILE SIZE 5G
BIGFILE DEFAULT TEMPORARY TABLESPACE temp01 TEMPFILE SIZE 500M;
```

Multiple Temporary Tablespaces

Beginning in Oracle 10^g, the database can be configured to use multiple default temporary tablespaces. This is accomplished using the new tablespace grouping mechanism. There is no explicit command for creating a tablespace group. Instead, when creating a temporary tablespace, you add the TABLESPACE GROUP clause to the CREATE TEMPORARY TABLESPACE or ALTER TABLESPACE commands. When you specify a group that did not previously exist, a new group is created. Thereafter, when you use the same name in another CREATE or ALTER command, the tablespace in question is added to the existing tablespace group. Tablespace groups share a namespace with tablespaces, so group names must not conflict with tablespace names.

Once a tablespace group has been created, the group name can be used in place of a tablespace name when assigning a default temporary tablespace for the database, or for a specific user. Some example commands are:

```
CREATE TEMPORARY TABLESPACE temp01 TEMPFILE SIZE 50M
  TABLESPACE GROUP tempgrp1;
```

```
ALTER TABLESPACE temp02 TABLESPACE GROUP tempgrp1;
```

```
ALTER DATABASE DEFAULT TEMPORARY TABLESPACE tempgrp1;
```

```
ALTER USER appowner TEMPORARY TABLESPACE tempgrp1;
```

Tablespaces can be added and removed from tablespace groups at will, using the ALTER TABLESPACE command. To move a tablespace to a different group, just use a different group name in the TABLESPACE GROUP clause. To remove a tablespace from a group, without moving it to a new group, use an empty string in the TABLESPACE GROUP clause as follows:

```
ALTER TABLESPACE temp02 TABLESPACE GROUP '';
```

When all tablespaces have been removed from a tablespace group, the group simply disappears. If a tablespace group is assigned as the database's default temporary tablespace, attempting to remove the last tablespace from the group will result in an error. Tablespace groups and their member tablespaces can be queried from the DBA_TABLESPACE_GROUPS view.

AUTOMATIC MEMORY TUNING

Two new parameters, WORKAREA_SIZE_POLICY and PGA_AGGREGATE_TARGET, were added in Oracle 9i release 1. If WORKAREA_SIZE_POLICY is set to TRUE and PGA_AGGREGATE_TARGET is set to a value greater than zero, Oracle will automatically allocate and deallocate memory from the memory regions of individual process global areas (PGAs). A PGA is a private memory area belonging to Oracle server processes, used to hold global variables, cursors, data structures, and process control information.

In previous releases, or when not using the new automatic PGA tuning ability, a DBA had to carefully tune the SORT_AREA_SIZE, HASH_AREA_SIZE, BITMAP_MERGE_AREA_SIZE, and CREATE_BITMAP_AREA_SIZE parameters to achieve optimal sort and join performance. Underallocation of these regions results in sort or join operations being done in multiple passes and increased disk activity due to temporary segment writes. Overallocation doesn't generate any performance problems directly, but it does rob available memory from other parts of Oracle, or from the operating system.

With automatic PGA tuning enabled, part of each PGA is still a fixed size, but the larger part is dynamically tunable by the database. As a process's needs shrink and grow, so does its PGA. This allows a smaller amount of memory to be allocated overall, since process A can shrink when process B needs to grow, and vice versa. The recommended starting point for PGA_AGGREGATE_TARGET on an online transaction processing (OLTP) system is 16% of physical memory, and for DSS systems, it is 40% of physical memory. This assumes you're only running a single database on the system in question, and that 20% of physical memory is left "free" for the OS and other needs. From that initial starting point, you can use the V$SQL_WORKAREA, V$SQL_WORKAREA_ACTIVE, V$PROCESS, and V$PGASTAT views to further tune the PGA_AGGREGATE_TARGET setting.

Oracle Corp's Metalink Note 223730.1 suggests querying the V$SQL_WORKAREA_ACTIVE view to determine if any PGA work areas are undersized, resulting in writes to temporary segments. The suggest query is:

```
SELECT
    to_number(decode(SID, 65535, NULL, SID)) sid,
    operation_type OPERATION,
    trunc(EXPECTED_SIZE/1024) ESIZE,
    trunc(ACTUAL_MEM_USED/1024) MEM,
    trunc(MAX_MEM_USED/1024) "MAX MEM",
    NUMBER_PASSES PASS,
```

```
   trunc(TEMPSEG_SIZE/1024) TSIZE
FROM
   V$SQL_WORKAREA_ACTIVE
ORDER BY 1,2;
```

The query lists the SID of each process; the type of operation being performed (e.g., group by, hash-join, etc.): expected, actual, and maximum memory usage; number of passes needed for the given operation; and the amount of temporary space used. Only active operations are listed in this query (and in the view it uses), and operations requiring significantly less than 64K of PGA are not listed, even when active.

Starting with Oracle 9*i* release 2, a view called V$PGA_TARGET_ADVICE is available. When the STATISTICS_LEVEL parameter is set to TYPICAL (the default) or ALL, this view is populated. The advice can be viewed using a query something like:

```
SELECT
   PGA_TARGET_FOR_ESTIMATE target,
   PGA_TARGET_FACTOR factor,
   ESTD_EXTRA_BYTES_RW extra_io,
   ESTD_PGA_CACHE_HIT_PERCENTAGE cache_hit,
   ESTD_OVERALLOC_COUNT overalloc
from
   v$pga_target_advice;
```

The query output lists a new suggested PGA target size, the factor by which the current target would be multiplied to achieve the new target, how much extra disk I/O (in blocks) would be required with the new setting, the estimated PGA cache hit ratio of the new setting, and the number of tasks that would be allocating more than their normal maximum PGA at the new setting. The goal is, of course, to have a cache hit ratio as close to 100% as possible, and to have zero processes overallocating their PGA. Obviously, it may not be possible to achieve the ideal numbers on some systems. Regardless, this advice view can help optimize this parameter.

Also starting with Oracle 9i, the different allocations of the SGA are dynamically tunable by the user. To enable this, a new parameter, called SGA_MAX_SIZE is available. If not set, SGA_MAX_SIZE defaults to the sum of the sizes of all the different pools in the SGA, such as buffer cache, shared pool, large pool, etc. If set manually, this parameter must equal or exceed its default value.

Dynamically tunable SGA can be very useful for systems that vary back and forth between OLTP and DSS. For example, an order entry system might be used interactively for 16 hours of the day, but spend its nights doing nothing but generating reports. In such cases, it might be best to reallocate some regions of the SGA at night, then return them to the OLTP settings during the day. For example, you might notice that your data buffer cache hit ratio drops at night while your shared pool appears to have more than enough random access memory (RAM). Using dynamic SGA settings, you can shrink the shared pool and grow the buffer cache using the following commands:

```
alter system set shared_pool_size = 1000M;
alter system set db_cache_size = 1500M;
```

When the night's reports are finished, you can move the memory back to the way it was using reciprocal commands:

```
alter system set shared_pool_size = 1000M;
alter system set db_cache_size = 1500M;
```

Once you've determined your system's needs at various times throughout the day, you can put them into batch files, shell scripts, or PL/SQL packages, and schedule them to execute at the appropriate times.

Starting with Oracle 10^g, the SGA becomes even more dynamic with the SGA_TARGET parameter. Setting SGA_TARGET to a non-zero value tells Oracle that it should adjust the DB_CACHE_SIZE, DB_nK_CACHE_SIZE, SHARED_POOL_SIZE, LARGE_POOL_SIZE, and JAVA_POOL_SIZE parameters at will. This eliminates the need for the DBA to spend a lot of time determining optimal sizes for various times of the day.

You can get information about SGA component sizes, and the resize operations on those components, by looking at the V$SGA_DYNAMIC_COMPONENTS and V$SGA_RESIZE_OPS views. The V$SGA_DYNAMIC_COMPONENTS view shows current, minimum, and maximum sizes of each component, plus information about the last resize operation performed on each. The V$SGA_RESIZE_OPS view shows a history of all resize operations since the database was started. Both manual and automatic resize operations are shown in both views.

SCHEDULING

Starting with Oracle 8, Oracle includes a fairly simple mechanism for scheduling tasks inside the database using DBMS_JOB. With the introduction of Oracle 10^g, Oracle adds the new DBMS_SCHEDULER command.

DBMS_JOB

To use the DBMS_JOB command, scheduled tasks must be coded as anonymous PL/SQL blocks, procedures, or packaged procedures. The scheduler is controlled via the DBMS_JOB package, and each user automatically has his/her own private job queue.

The main procedures used from the DBMS_JOB package are listed in Table 4-1:

Table 4-1 DBMS_JOB Procedures

Procedure	Description
SUBMIT	Submits a job to the queue.
REMOVE	Removes an existing job from the queue.

Table 4-1 DBMS_JOB Procedures (continued)

Procedure	Description
CHANGE	Alters one or more attributes of a queued job. The job's task, next execution time, or interval between executions can be modified with this procedure.
WHAT	Alters the task to be executed by a queued job.
NEXT_DATE	Alters the next execution time of a queued job.
INTERVAL	Alters the interval between executions of a queued job.
BROKEN	Marks a queued job as broken or unbroken, depending on arguments. When a job is marked as broken, the scheduler will not try to execute it, regardless of execution time or interval settings.
RUN	Forces a queued job to run.

Submitting a Job

When submitting a job to the queue, you must, at minimum, specify what is to be run (WHAT), and the time it is to be run (NEXT_DATE). If the job is a recurring one, you must also supply an argument indicating the interval (INTERVAL) at which the job run is to be repeated. The DBMS_JOB.SUBMIT procedure has one output parameter, so you must supply a variable to receive that value. In SQL Plus, submitting a job is done as follows:

```
VAR jobno NUMBER
BEGIN
DBMS_JOB.SUBMIT ( :jobno,
'MY_PACKAGE.MY_PROCEDURE ( ''ARG1'' ) ;',
  SYSDATE,
  'SYSDATE+1' ) ;
  COMMIT;
END;
/
```

In this example, the task submitted is the MY_PROCEDURE procedure from the MY_PACKAGE package. A VARCHAR2 argument is provided, with a value of 'ARG1'. The job is initially scheduled to run immediately, and is to be repeated roughly every 24 hours (SYSDATE+1). The job will not begin running until a commit is issued.

Removing a Job

The DBMS_JOB.REMOVE procedure only has one required argument: the ID of an existing job. You can find the ID by querying the USER_JOBS view:

```
SELECT job, what FROM user_jobs;
```

Once the ID is obtained, the job can easily be removed:

```
BEGIN
  DBMS_JOB.REMOVE(1234);
END;
/
```

You can only remove jobs that you own. Jobs that are executing when removed will immediately stop showing in the USER_JOBS view, but will continue to execute until they are finished.

Altering a Job

Currently queued jobs can be modified with the CHANGE, WHAT, NEXT_DATE, or INTERVAL procedures of the DBMS_JOB package.

DBMS_JOB.CHANGE

The CHANGE procedure takes four arguments: job ID, what is to be run, the next date at which it is to be run, and the interval at which it is to be repeated. The ID must not be null and must match a job already in the queue. Any or all of the other three arguments may be null. A null argument leaves that setting unchanged. An example is:

```
BEGIN

    DBMS_JOB.CHANGE( 1234,

    'MY_PACKAGE.MY_PROCEDURE( ''ARG2'' );',

    NULL,

    'SYSDATE+.5' );

END;

/
```

This example tells job `1234` to execute `MY_PACKAGE`'s `MY_PROCEDURE` with an argument of `'ARG2'`, and that it should be repeated roughly every 12 hours. The time of the next scheduled execution is unchanged.

DBMS_JOB.WHAT, DBMS_JOB.NEXT_DATE and DBMS_JOB.INTERVAL

The other three job alteration procedures are subsets of the `CHANGE` procedure and each changes only one setting at a time. Examples are:

```
BEGIN

    DBMS_JOB.WHAT( 1234, 'MY_PACKAGE.MY_PROCEDURE( ''ARG3'' );' );

END;

/

BEGIN

    DBMS_JOB.NEXT_DATE( 1234, SYSDATE+.25 );
```

```
END;
/
BEGIN
    DBMS_JOB.INTERVAL ( 1234,  'TRUNC(SYSDATE)+1' ) ;
END;
/
```

The first example changes what is to be run to 'ARG3'. The second example tells the schedule that the job's next run should start in 6 hours (current time plus .25 days). The third example says that the job should be repeated every 24 hours, starting exactly at midnight.

Broken Jobs

If a running job exits abnormally by throwing a PL/SQL exception, the scheduler records the error and continues retrying at the indicated interval until the job has errored out a total of 16 times. After 16 errors, the job is marked as broken and will not be retried without user intervention.

You can find out what error the job is throwing by looking in the database's alert log. Once the error has been corrected, you can restart the job by resetting its broken status as follows:

```
BEGIN
    DBMS_JOB.BROKEN( 1234, FALSE ) ;
END;
/
```

To cause a job to stop running without unscheduling it, you can use the BROKEN procedure with a TRUE value for the second argument. The only catch is that if the job is running when the BROKEN procedure is executed, a successful finish will reset the job to an unbroken status.

A broken job can also be set to unbroken by successfully forcing it to run with the DBMS_JOB.RUN procedure, which is discussed next.

Forcing a Job to Run

You can use the DBMS_JOB.RUN procedure to force a job to run, even if it's marked as broken. The syntax is very simple:

```
BEGIN
    DBMS_JOB.RUN( 1234 ) ;
END;
/
```

The RUN procedure causes the job to be scheduled immediately, regardless of its broken status. The job is run in the current session, and the command won't return until the job has completed. The next execution date will be recalculated based on the current time. That means, if the job is scheduled to run every seven days, and you successfully execute the DBMS_JOB.RUN command on a Thursday, the next execution will be on the following Thursday.

Forcibly Terminating a Running Job

The DBA_JOBS_RUNNING view shows specific information about jobs that are currently being executed. To kill a running job completely, first mark it as broken using DBMS_JOB.BROKEN, then use ALTER SYSTEM KILL SESSION command to disconnect its session. The following query can be used to find the necessary information:

```
SELECT
    s.sid,
    s.serial#,
    r.job,
    j.what
FROM
    dba_jobs_running r,
    v$session s,
    dba_jobs j
```

```
WHERE
     r.job = j.job AND
     r.sid = s.sid;
```

DBMS_SCHEDULER

Starting with Oracle 10^g, task scheduling can (and should) be done with the DBMS_SCHEDULER package, rather than DBMS_JOB. While perfectly serviceable for simple tasks, the DBMS_JOB package lacks the flexibility needed to really model business processes in a database.

As with DBMS_JOB, the DBMS_SCHEDULER package can run specified jobs at specified intervals, repeating forever. Unlike the older tool, the scheduler can also go far beyond that. Scheduled tasks can be grouped, prioritized, and resource-limited. You can even set blackout periods during which no tasks should be run. The capabilities of the new scheduler are vastly improved.

The scheduler uses three basic "elements" for scheduling: programs, schedules, and jobs. A program is essentially the equivalent of the WHAT setting on DBMS_JOB; a schedule is very roughly equivalent to the NEXT_DATE and INTERVAL settings in DBMS_JOB; and a job is a user-defined task that combines a program and a schedule into an actual executable element. A job can be created independently using the simple job application programming interface (API), or it can combine existing programs and schedules.

Every time a job runs, a job instance is created. A job that is scheduled to run only once will have only a single job instance, but a recurring job will generate a new job instance with every execution. The actual job will only show up once in the job queue, but each instance of the job will show up separately in the job log.

For the convenience of scheduling and resource management, jobs can be grouped into job classes. Setting the attributes of a job class will set defaults for all jobs that exist within the class. These defaults can still be overridden on a job-by-job basis. Jobs can also be prioritized within a job class so that higher priority jobs will always run before lower priority jobs. A job can only be a member of a single job class, and a job class can't be dropped until all jobs have been removed from that class.

The scheduler also supports "windows" to allow you to manage resource allocation during specific time intervals. Each window has a duration, a schedule, a resource plan, and a priority. You should not schedule windows so that they overlap, but if they do, the highest priority window takes precedence.

You can also group windows for simplicity. An example would be to create a group of windows to define all of your scheduled downtime, so that maintenance jobs requiring downtime could be scheduled to run only during those windows.

Creating a Program

Stored program definitions are created with the CREATE_PROGRAM procedure of the DBMS_SCHEDULER package. A program is given a name that uniquely identifies it and that must be unique within the SQL namespace. That is to say, a program can't have the same name as a table or index.

A program can be defined as a PLSQL_BLOCK, STORED_PROCEDURE, or EXECUTABLE. A PLSQL_BLOCK is an anonymous block that takes no arguments. A program defined as a STORED_PROCEDURE can have arguments of any type supported by the scheduler. An EXECUT-ABLE program indicates that the scheduler is to run a program that's external to the database. The type of arguments that can be specified for an EXECUTABLE program are somewhat restricted. An example program definition is:

```
BEGIN
DBMS_SCHEDULER.CREATE_PROGRAM(
    program_name => 'my_program',
    program_type => 'stored_procedure',
    program_action => 'MY_PACKAGE.MY_PROCEDURE',
    number_of_arguments => 3,
    enabled => TRUE,
    comments => 'Insert clever comment here' );
```

END;

/

When a program is created with the number_of_arguments parameter set to anything greater than zero, you must define those arguments before the program can be used. Arguments are defined with the DEFINE_PROGRAM_ARGUMENT, DEFINE_PROGRAM_ANYDATA_ARGUMENT, and DEFINE_METADATA_ARGUMENT procedures. To continue the example:

```
BEGIN
  DBMS_SCHEDULER.DEFINE_PROGRAM_ARGUMENT (
    program_name => 'my_program',
    argument_name => 'first_arg',
    argument_position => 1, /* starts with 1, not zero */
    argument_type => 'VARCHAR2', /* info only, not checked */
    argument_default_value => 'first argument default value',
    out_argument => FALSE );

  DBMS_SCHEDULER.DEFINE_PROGRAM_ANYDATA_ARGUMENT (
    program_name => 'my_program',
    argument_name => 'second_arg',
    argument_position => 2,
    argument_type => 'NUMBER', /* info only, not checked */
```

```
    argument_default_value => SYS.ANYDATA.ConvertNumber(5.035),
    out_argument => FALSE );

DBMS_SCHEDULER.DEFINE_METADATA_ARGUMENT (
    program_name => 'my_program',
    argument_name => 'third_arg',
    argument_position => 3,
    argument_name => 'window_end' );

END;
/
```

Any argument that isn't or can't be represented as a VARCHAR2 must be defined using the DEFINE_PROGRAM_ANYDATA_ARGUMENT procedure. The out_argument parameter must currently be set to FALSE, which is the default, though this will probably change in future releases.

The DEFINE_METADATA_ARGUMENT procedure is something of a special case. Since it can be useful for a program to know about its environment when it is executed, you can pass a number of pre-defined metadata arguments to any STORED_PROCEDURE or EXECUTABLE. The available arguments are JOB_NAME, JOB_OWNER, JOB_START, WINDOW_START, and WINDOW_END. Each metadata argument can only be passed once to a given program.

Altering a Program

After it has been created, a program's definition can be changed using the SET_ATTRIBUTE or SET_ATTRIBUTE_NULL procedure. These procedures are generically used to alter jobs and schedules, as well as programs.

The SET_ATTRIBUTE_NULL procedure sets a designated attribute to NULL, if NULL is an allowable value for the attribute in question. If the program is enabled, it is disabled, the attribute is set to NULL, and the program is re-enabled. If the object can't be re-enabled, an error is generated, and the program is left disabled.

```
BEGIN

DBMS_SCHEDULER.SET_ATTRIBUTE (

  name => 'my_program',

  attribute => 'program_action',

  value => 'MY_PACKAGE.MY_PROCEDURE2' );


DBMS_SCHEDULER.SET_ATTRIBUTE_NULL (

  name => 'my_program',

  attribute => 'comments' );

END;

/
```

Dropping a Program

You can use the DROP_PROGRAM procedure to drop one or more programs at a time. To drop more than one program, the program_name argument to this procedure should be a comma-delimited list of program names. For example:

```
BEGIN
DBMS_SCHEDULER.DROP_PROGRAM(
program_name => 'my_prog1, my_prog2, my_prog3',
force => FALSE );
END;
/
```

If there are any jobs pointing to the program when you attempt to drop it, an error will be generated unless you specify TRUE for the value of the force argument. If the drop is forced, any jobs pointing to the dropped program will be disabled. Running jobs that point to the program are not affected and will continue to run. Any arguments associated with the program will be dropped along with it.

Disabling a Program

The DISABLE procedure can be used to disable a program, job, or window group. Multiple programs can be disabled at the same time by specifying a comma-delimited list of program names as the value of the name argument.

```
BEGIN
   DBMS_SCHEDULER.DISABLE (
      program_name => 'my_prog1, my_prog2, my_prog3 ' ,
      force => FALSE ) ;
END;
/
```

As with dropping a program, an error will be generated if there are jobs pointing to it and the force argument is set to FALSE. Unlike the DROP_PROGRAM procedure, forcing a program to disabled will not disable associated jobs.

Enabling a Program

Just as a program is disabled with the DISABLE procedure, it is enabled with the ENABLE procedure. Again, multiple programs can be enabled at the same time, by specifying a comma-delimited list of programs as the value of the name argument.

```
BEGIN
   DBMS_SCHEDULER.ENABLE (
      program_name => 'my_prog1, my_prog2, my_prog3 ' ) ;
END;
/
```

Creating a Schedule

Stored schedule definitions are created with the CREATE_SCHEDULE procedure. A start date in DBMS_SCHEDULER terms does not mean the same thing as it does in DBMS_JOB. For a non-repeating schedule, the start date indicates when the job should run. For a repeating schedule, it specifies when the REPEAT_INTERVAL becomes valid, and is used as a reference date to determine the first run time.

```
BEGIN
DBMS_SCHEDULER.CREATE_SCHEDULE (
    schedule_name => 'my_sched1',
    start_date => '31-DEC-04 12.00.00.000000 AM -06:00',
    repeat_interval => 'FREQ=HOURLY;INTERVAL=3',
    end_date => '31-DEC-05 12.00.00.000000 AM -06:00' );
END;
/
```

You can create schedules in your own schema or in another schema with proper privileges. Once created, access to schedules is automatically granted to PUBLIC so others can use your schedules.

Altering a Schedule

With the exception of a schedule's name, all of its attributes can be modified after it is created. As with programs, schedules are altered with the SET_ATTRIBUTE and SET_ATTRIBUTE_NULL procedures.

SET_ATTRIBUTE_NULL is used to set a schedule attribute to null. If the attribute in question is not nullable, an error will be generated.

```
BEGIN
  DBMS_SCHEDULER.SET_ATTRIBUTE (
    name => 'my_schedule',
    attribute => 'end_date',
    value => '31-DEC-06 12.00.00.000000 AM -06:00' );

  DBMS_SCHEDULER.SET_ATTRIBUTE_NULL(
    name => 'my_schedule',
    attribute => 'comments' );

END;
/
```

Dropping a Schedule

Schedules are dropped with the DROP_SCHEDULE procedure. You can drop several schedules at a time by specifying a comma-delimited list of schedules as the value of the SCHEDULE_NAME parameter.

```
BEGIN
 DBMS_SCHEDULER.DROP_SCHEDULE (
  schedule_name => 'my_sched1, my_sched2, my_sched3',
  force => FALSE );
END;
/
```

If force is set to FALSE, and any jobs or windows are pointing to this schedule, an error will be generated. If set to TRUE, any jobs or windows pointing to the schedule will be disabled and the schedule will be dropped.

Creating a Job

The DBMS_SCHEDULER.CREATE_JOB procedure is used to create jobs. When creating a job, both the action to be performed and the schedule on which it is to be performed must be specified.

In its basic form, the CREATE_JOB procedure doesn't require any predefined programs or schedules. For example:

```
BEGIN
  DBMS_SCHEDULER.CREATE_JOB(
    job_name => 'my_job1',
    job_type => 'PLSQL_BLOCK',
    job_action => 'DELETE FROM act_log WHERE act_time < sysdate-30;',
    start_date => '31-DEC-04 12.00.00.000000 AM -06:00',
    repeat_interval => 'FREQ=HOURLY;INTERVAL=3',
    end_date => '31-DEC-05 12.00.00.000000 AM -06:00' );
END;
/
```

This example creates a job to delete data older than 30 days from the act_log table. The job runs every three hours, starting on the last day of 2004 and ending on the last day of 2005.

At the other extreme, CREATE_JOB can use predefined schedules and programs:

```
BEGIN
  DBMS_SCHEDULER.CREATE_JOB(
    job_name => 'my_job2',
    program_name => 'my_program',
    schedule_name => 'my_schedule' );
```

```
END;
/
```

CREATE_JOB is also overloaded such that you can create jobs with a predefined program and an ad-hoc schedule, and vice-versa:

```
BEGIN

DBMS_SCHEDULER.CREATE_JOB(

    job_name => 'my_job3',

    program_name => 'my_program',

    start_date => '31-DEC-04 12.00.00.000000 AM -06:00',

    repeat_interval => 'FREQ=HOURLY;INTERVAL=3',

    end_date => '31-DEC-05 12.00.00.000000 AM -06:00' );


DBMS_SCHEDULER.CREATE_JOB(

    job_name => 'my_job4',

    schedule_name => 'my_schedule',

    job_type => 'PLSQL_BLOCK',

    job_action => 'DELETE FROM act_log WHERE act_time < sysdate-30;',

    number_of_arguments => 0 );

END;
/
```

Jobs are, by default, set to disabled when they are created, and need to be enabled before they will run. As soon as it is scheduled, a job's information can be queried from the `*_SCHEDULER_JOBS` views.

Unlike with `DBMS_JOB`, `DBMS_SCHEDULER` jobs can be created in another schema by simply specifying `'schema_name.name'` for the `job_name` parameter. Regardless of who created the job, it is executed with the privileges of the schema in which it was created, just as if it had been created by that schema owner.

If you create a job using an inline (not predefined) program that requires arguments, or if you wish to override a predefined job's default arguments, you'll need to set the job arguments using either the `SET_JOB_ARGUMENT_VALUE` or `SET_JOB_ANYDATA_VALUE` procedure. There is no `METADATA` procedure specific to jobs since it wouldn't make sense to override a derived argument.

```
BEGIN
    DBMS_SCHEDULER.SET_JOB_ARGUMENT_VALUE (
        job_name => 'my_job2',
        argument_position => 1, /* starts with 1, not zero */
        argument_value => 'first argument actual value' );

    DBMS_SCHEDULER.DEFINE_PROGRAM_ANYDATA_ARGUMENT (
        job_name => 'my_job2',
```

```
  argument_position => 2,
  argument_value => SYS.ANYDATA.ConvertNumber(16.8) );
END;
/
```

To set a job's argument back to its default value, use the RESET_JOB_ARGUMENT procedure. If you reset an argument that has no default value defined, the job will be disabled.

```
BEGIN
  DBMS_SCHEDULER.RESET_JOB_ARGUMENT  (
    job_name => 'my_job2',
    argument_position => 1 );
END;
/
```

Copying a Job

The COPY_JOB procedure copies an existing job to a new job. The new job is created as disabled, and is identical to the old job except for its name.

```
BEGIN
  DBMS_SCHEDULER.COPY_JOB  (
    old_job => 'my_job2',
```

```
  new_job => 'my_job5' );

END;
/
```

Altering a Job

As with programs and schedules, jobs are altered using the SET_ATTRIBUTE and SET_ATTRIBUTE_NULL procedures.

The SET_ATTRIBUTE_NULL procedure sets a designated attribute to NULL, if NULL is an allowable value for the attribute in question. If the job is enabled, it is disabled, the attribute is set to NULL, and the job is re-enabled. If the object can't be re-enabled, an error is generated, and the job is left disabled.

```
BEGIN
  DBMS_SCHEDULER.SET_ATTRIBUTE (
    name => 'my_job1',
    attribute => 'job_action',
    value => 'DELETE FROM act_log WHERE act_time < sysdate-45;' );

  DBMS_SCHEDULER.SET_ATTRIBUTE_NULL (
    name => 'my_job1',
    attribute => 'comments' );

END;
/
```

Running a Job Manually

In spite of the flexibility of the DBMS_SCHEDULER package, there may still be occasions for which the user wants to run a schedule job immediately and synchronously. This can be accomplished with the RUN_JOB procedure:

```
BEGIN
  DBMS_SCHEDULER.RUN_JOB( job_name => 'my_job1' );
END;
/
```

Stopping a Job

A running job can be stopped with the STOP_JOB procedure. After being stopped, a one-time job will be set to STOPPED, and will not automatically run again. A recurring job will have a SCHEDULED status, and will run again at its next scheduled time.

The STOP_JOB procedure takes a single job name or job class name, or a list of jobs and/or job classes as the value for its job_name parameter. Since job classes always reside in the SYS schema, they should be preceded with "sys".

```
BEGIN
  DBMS_SCHEDULER.STOP_JOB (
    job_name => 'my_job1, my_job2, sys.my_job_class1',
    force => false ) ;
END;
/
```

When force is set to FALSE (the default), the job will be stopped by the equivalent of sending it a Ctrl-C. If this fails, the job will continue to run and an error will be returned. If force is set to TRUE, the job is first sent a Ctrl-C in an attempt to terminate it gracefully. If the graceful option fails, the job slave process is terminated.

Dropping a Job

Jobs are dropped using the DROP_JOB procedure. When a job is dropped, it's removed from the job queue. If an instance of the job is running when DROP_JOB is called, an error is returned, unless the force parameter is set to TRUE. If force is TRUE, the job is first stopped, then dropped.

As with the STOP_JOB procedure, the job_name parameter will accept a single job or job class, or a comma-delimited list of jobs and/or job classes.

```
BEGIN
  DBMS_SCHEDULER.DROP_JOB(
    job_name => 'my_job1, my_job2, sys.my_job_class1',
    force => false );
END;
/
```

Disabling a Job

Jobs are disabled using the DISABLE procedure. When a job is disabled, it remains in the job queue with its state set to DISABLED. If an instance of the job is running when DISABLE is called, an error is returned, unless force is set to TRUE. If force is TRUE, the job is first stopped, then disabled.

As with the STOP_JOB procedure, the job_name parameter will accept a single job or job class, or a comma-delimited list of jobs and/or job classes.

```
BEGIN
  DBMS_SCHEDULER.DISABLE(
    name => 'my_job1, my_job2, sys.my_job_class1',
    force => false );
END;
/
```

Enabling a Job

Jobs are enabled using the ENABLE procedure. When a job is enabled, it remains in the job queue with its state set to ENABLED.

As with the STOP_JOB procedure, the job_name parameter will accept a single job or job class, or a comma-delimited list of jobs and/or job classes.

```
BEGIN
DBMS_SCHEDULER.ENABLE (
  name => 'my_job1, my_job2, sys.my_job_class1' );
END;
/
```

Creating a Job Class

Job classes are created using the CREATE_JOB_CLASS procedure. Job classes always belong to the SYS schema.

```
BEGIN
DBMS_SCHEDULER.CREATE_JOB_CLASS (
  job_class_name => 'my_job_class1',
  logging_level => DBMS_SCHEDULER.LOGGING_RUNS,
  log_history => 10 );
END;
/
```

This example creates a job class named my_job_class1. Its member jobs will, by default, log a medium level of information, and that log data will be retained for 10 days.

Altering a Job Class

As with programs, schedules, and jobs, job classes are altered using the SET_ATTRIBUTE and SET_ATTRIBUTE_NULL procedures.

The SET_ATTRIBUTE_NULL procedure sets a designated attribute to NULL, if NULL is an allowable value for the attribute in question.

```
BEGIN
DBMS_SCHEDULER.SET_ATTRIBUTE (
    name => 'my_job_class1',
    attribute => 'service',
    value => 'RAC_service1' );

DBMS_SCHEDULER.SET_ATTRIBUTE_NULL (
    name => 'my_job_class1',
    attribute => 'comments' );
END;
/
```

Dropping a Job Class

The DROP_JOB_CLASS procedure is used to drop job classes. If any jobs belong to the class, any attempt to drop the class will result in an error, unless force is set to TRUE. If force is TRUE, the job class is dropped, and all members belonging to that class are disabled and moved to the default class.

Multiple job classes can be dropped in a single call by setting the value of the job_class_name argument to a comma-delimited list of job class names.

```
BEGIN
DBMS_SCHEDULER.DROP_JOB_CLASS (
    job_class_name => 'my_job_class1, my_job_class2',
    force => FALSE ) ;
END;
/
```

Creating a Window

Windows are created with the CREATE_WINDOW procedure. When creating a window, you can optionally set the window's schedule. The schedule can be set using a predefined schedule object or an inline (not predefined) schedule. As with job classes, all windows are created in the SYS schema.

```
BEGIN
  -- Using a predefined schedule
  DBMS_SCHEDULER.CREATE_WINDOW(
    window_name => 'my_window',
    schedule_name => 'my_schedule',
    resource_plan => 'my_resource_plan',
    duration => interval '60' minute );

  -- Using an inline schedule
  DBMS_SCHEDULER.CREATE_WINDOW(
    window_name => 'my_window',
    resource_plan => 'my_resource_plan',
    start_date => '01-DEC-03 10.00.00.000000 AM -06:00',
    repeat_interval => 'FREQ=WEEKLY; BYDAY=FRI;',
    duration => interval '60' minute );
END;
/
```

Altering a Window

As with all other scheduler objects, windows are altered using the SET_ATTRIBUTE and SET_ATTRIBUTE_NULL procedures.

The SET_ATTRIBUTE_NULL procedure sets a designated attribute to NULL, if NULL is an allowable value for the attribute in question. If the window is enabled, it is disabled, the attribute is set to NULL, and the window is re-enabled. If the object can't be re-enabled, an error is generated, and the window is left disabled.

```
BEGIN
  DBMS_SCHEDULER.SET_ATTRIBUTE (
    name => 'my_window',
    attribute => 'window_priority',
    value => 'LOW' );

  DBMS_SCHEDULER.SET_ATTRIBUTE_NULL (
    name => 'my_window',
    attribute => 'comments' );

END;
/
```

Opening a Window

Normally, windows open on their own based on the schedule defined with CREATE_WINDOW or SET_ATTRIBUTE. If desired, a window can be opened manually using the OPEN_WINDOW procedure.

If you attempt to open a window while another window is already open, an error will be returned, unless force is set to TRUE. If force is TRUE, the previously open window will be closed, and the window designated in the OPEN_WINDOW call will be opened.

When opening a window manually, you can specify a duration in the OPEN_WINDOW call. When the window closes, the window priority algorithm is applied to determine what, if any, window should be opened at that time.

```
BEGIN
DBMS_SCHEDULER.OPEN_WINDOW (
    window_name => 'my_window',
    duration => INTERVAL '30' MINUTE,
    force => FALSE ) ;

END;
/
```

Closing a Window

Normally, windows close on their own, based on the schedule defined with CREATE_WINDOW or SET_ATTRIBUTE. If desired, a window can be closed manually using the CLOSE_WINDOW procedure. When the window closes, the window priority algorithm is applied to determine what, if any, window should be opened at that time.

Jobs scheduled by the window, which are running when the window closes, will not stop unless the job's stop_on_window_close argument is set to TRUE. Jobs scheduled by the window's window group will not close when the window closes if another window in the same group immediately opens, even if stop_on_window_close is set to TRUE.

```
BEGIN
    DBMS_SCHEDULER.CLOSE_WINDOW( window_name => 'my_window' ) ;
END;
/
```

Dropping a Window

Windows are dropped by invoking the DROP_WINDOW procedure. When a window is dropped, all references to it are removed from any associated window groups.

Multiple windows can be dropped by providing a comma-delimited list of windows or window group names as the value of the `window_name` parameter. Note that if window group names are supplied, all windows in the group are dropped, but the window group itself remains.

Attempting to drop an open window will result in an error, unless `force` is set to TRUE. If `force` is TRUE, the window will be closed, then dropped. Note that if the window is closed, the normal window priority algorithm will be applied to determine if any other window should be immediately opened.

If there are jobs that have the window as their schedule, then the window drop will fail with an error unless `force` is set to TRUE. If `force` is TRUE, the job(s) will be disabled. Running jobs that have the dropped window as their schedule will be allowed to continue unless `stop_on_window_close` is set to TRUE.

Disabling a Window

The `DISABLE` procedure can be used to disable a window. Disabled windows will never open, but will remain available.

Attempting to disable an open window will result in an error, unless the `force` parameter is set to TRUE. If `force` is TRUE, then the window will be closed, then disabled. Note that if the window is closed, the normal window priority algorithm will be applied to determine if any other window should be immediately opened.

If there are jobs that have the window as their schedule, the window disable will fail with an error, unless force is set to TRUE. If force is TRUE, the window will be disabled, but its associated job(s) will remain enabled.

One or more windows or window groups can be disabled in a single DISABLE call if a comma-delimited list of windows and window groups is provided as the value of the name parameter. Since all windows and window groups belong to the SYS schema, and DISABLE is used to disable multiple scheduler object types, all window and window group names should be preceded by "sys".

```
BEGIN
DBMS_SCHEDULER.DISABLE(
    name => 'sys.my_window1, sys.my_window_group1',
    force => false );
END;
/
```

Enabling a Window

The ENABLE procedure can be used to enable a window. When attempting to enable a window, a validity check is performed before the window is actually enabled. If the check fails, the window will remain disabled and the ENABLE call will return an error.

One or more windows or window groups can be enabled in a single ENABLE call if a comma-delimited list of windows and window groups is provided as the value of the name attribute. Since all windows and window groups belong to the SYS schema, and ENABLE is used to enable multiple scheduler object types, all window and window group names should be preceded by "sys".

```
BEGIN
DBMS_SCHEDULER.ENABLE (
  name => 'sys.my_window1, sys.my_window_group1' ) ;
END;
/
```

Creating a Window Group

The CREATE_WINDOW_GROUP procedure is used to create window groups. A window group can have one or more windows as members, and only windows can be members. Member windows can be specified at create time or can be added later. A window group can't be a member of another window group, but a window group may have no members at all. As with windows, window groups are always created in the SYS schema.

```
BEGIN
DBMS_SCHEDULER.CREATE_WINDOW_GROUP (
  group_name => 'my_window_group',
  window_list => 'my_window1, my_window2' ) ;
```

END;

/

Dropping a Window Group

Window groups are dropped with the DROP_WINDOW_GROUP procedure. Dropping a window group that has member windows will drop only the window group itself. None of the member windows will be dropped.

If there are jobs that have the window group as their schedule, then the drop will fail with an error, unless force is set to TRUE. If force is TRUE, the job or jobs will be disabled. Running jobs that have the dropped window group as their schedule will be allowed to continue, even if stop_on_window_close is set to TRUE.

A window group can be dropped successfully even if one of its member windows is open when the DROP command is issued.

Adding a Window to a Window Group

Windows are added using the ADD_WINDOW_GROUP_MEMBER procedure. The scheduler only checks for jobs scheduled by a window when a window opens, so adding a window to a group will generally have no immediate effect on running jobs.

If a newly created job points to the new window, it will not be started until the next time the window opens.

```
BEGIN
  DBMS_SCHEDULER.ADD_WINDOW_GROUP_MEMBER (
    group_name  => 'my_window_group',
    window_list => 'my_window3, my_window4' ) ;
END;
/
```

Dropping a Window from a Window Group

Windows are dropped from a window group using the REMOVE_WINDOW_GROUP_MEMBER procedure. Dropping an open window from a window group has no effect on running jobs.

```
BEGIN
  DBMS_SCHEDULER.REMOVE_WINDOW_GROUP_MEMBER (
    group_name  => 'my_window_group',
    window_list => 'my_window3, my_window4' ) ;
END;
/
```

Disabling a Window Group

The `DISABLE` procedure can be used to disable a window group. Disabled window groups will never open, but their member windows will continue to open and close as normal.

Attempting to disable a window group while one of its members is open will result in an error, unless `force` is set to TRUE. If `force` is TRUE, the window group will be disabled, but the open member window will not be closed, and will continue normally.

If there are jobs that have the window group as their schedule, then the window disable will fail with an error, unless force is set to TRUE. If `force` is TRUE, the window group will be disabled, but its associated job(s) will remain enabled.

One or more windows or window groups can be disabled in a single `DISABLE` call if a comma-delim-ited list of windows and window groups is provided as the value of the `name` parameter. Since all windows and window groups belong to the **SYS** schema, and `DISABLE` is used to disable multiple scheduler object types, all window and window group names should be preceded by "sys".

```
BEGIN
DBMS_SCHEDULER.DISABLE (
    name => 'sys.my_window1, sys.my_window_group1',
    force => false );
END;
/
```

Enabling a Window Group

The ENABLE procedure can be used to enable a window. Enabling a window group does not enable its associated windows.

One or more windows or window groups can be enabled in a single ENABLE call if a comma-delimited list of windows and window groups is provided as the value of the name parameter. Since all windows and window groups belong to the SYS schema, and ENABLE is used to enable multiple scheduler object types, all window and window group names should be preceded by "sys".

```
BEGIN

DBMS_SCHEDULER.ENABLE (

    name => 'sys.my_window1, sys.my_window_group1' );

END;
/
```

SCHEDULING REFERENCE

This section defines some of the most common and/or important scheduling parameters. Each parameter is in its own section, and each section begins with a syntax example and a table of the properties of the parameter, and has a description of how the parameter is used following the table.

DBMS_JOB

SUBMIT

```
DBMS_JOB.SUBMIT(
job     OUT BINARY_INTEGER,
what        IN VARCHAR2,
next_date IN DATE DEFAULT sysdate,
interval IN VARCHAR2 DEFAULT 'null',
no_parse IN BOOLEAN DEFAULT FALSE,
instance IN BINARY_INTEGER DEFAULT any_instance,
force     IN BOOLEAN DEFAULT FALSE ) ;
```

Table 4-2 DBMS_JOB.SUBMIT Parameters

Parameter	Description
job	Returns the number assigned to the submitted job. Assigned from the sys.jobseq sequence.
what	Defines the body of the PL/SQL block to be run.
next_date	Indicates the initial run time.
interval	Gives a PL/SQL expression, to be used to calculate subsequent run times.

Table 4-2 DBMS_JOB.SUBMIT Parameters (continued)

Parameter	Description
no_parse	If this flag is set to FALSE, the WHAT block is parsed immediately. If set to TRUE the block is parsed just before the first run.
instance	Specifies which instance in a cluster is to run the job. If set to DBMS_JOB.ANY_INSTANCE, any instance can run the job.
force	If set to TRUE, any integer can be specified for the INSTANCE argument. If set to FALSE, the specified instance must be running or the SUBMIT call will fail.

The SUBMIT procedure creates a new entry in the calling user's job queue. The instance and force parameters allow the user to create a job with affinity to a particular cluster node.

REMOVE

```
DBMS_JOB.REMOVE (
    job     IN BINARY_INTEGER ) ;
```

Table 4-3   DBMS_JOB.REMOVE Parameter

Parameter	Description
job	Indicates the number of the job to be removed.

The REMOVE procedure drops an existing entry from the calling user's job queue.

CHANGE

```
DBMS_JOB.CHANGE(
    job      IN BINARY_INTEGER,
    what     IN VARCHAR2,
    next_date IN DATE DEFAULT sysdate,
    interval IN VARCHAR2 DEFAULT 'null',
    instance IN BINARY_INTEGER DEFAULT any_instance,
    force    IN BOOLEAN DEFAULT FALSE );
```

Table 4-4 DBMS_JOB.CHANGE Parameters

Parameter	Description
job	Indicates the number of the job to be changed.
what	Defines the body of the PL/SQL block to be run.
next_date	Indicates the initial run time.
interval	Gives a PL/SQL expression, to be used to calculate subsequent run times.

Table 4-4 DBMS_JOB.CHANGE Parameters (continued)

Parameter	Description
no_parse	If this flag is set to FALSE, the WHAT block is parsed immediately. If set to TRUE, the block is parsed just before the first run.
instance	Specifies which instance in a cluster is to run the job. If set to DBMS_JOB.ANY_INSTANCE, any instance can run the job.
force	If set to TRUE, any integer can be specified for the INSTANCE argument. If set to FALSE, the specified instance must be running or the SUBMIT call will fail.

The CHANGE procedure alters an existing entry in the calling user's job queue. The instance and force parameters allow the user to create a job with affinity to a particular cluster node.

If the WHAT, NEXT_DATE, or INTERVAL parameters are NULL, the CHANGE procedure leaves that part of the job's existing definition as-is.

WHAT

```
DBMS_JOB.WHAT (
job     IN BINARY_INTEGER,
next_date IN DATE DEFAULT sysdate ) ;
```

Table 4-5 DBMS_JOB. WHAT Parameters

Parameter	Description
job	Indicates the number of the job to be changed.
what	Defines the body of the PL/SQL block to be run.

The WHAT procedure alters the PL/SQL block of an existing entry in the calling user's job queue.

NEXT_DATE

```
DBMS_JOB.NEXT_DATE (
job     IN BINARY_INTEGER,
what    IN VARCHAR2 ) ;
```

Table 4-6   DBMS_JOB.NEXT_DATE Parameters

Parameter	Description
job	Indicates the number of the job to be changed.
next_date	Indicates the initial run time.

The NEXT_DATE procedure alters the next run time of an existing entry in the calling user's job queue.

INSTANCE

```
DBMS_JOB.INSTANCE(
job     IN BINARY_INTEGER,
instance IN BINARY_INTEGER DEFAULT any_instance,
force   IN BOOLEAN DEFAULT FALSE );
```

Table 4-7 DBMS_JOB.INSTANCE Parameters

Parameter	Description
job	Indicates the number of the job to be changed.
instance	Specifies which instance in a cluster is to run the job. If set to DBMS_JOB.ANY_INSTANCE, any instance can run the job.
force	If set to TRUE, any integer can be specified for the INSTANCE argument. If set to FALSE, the specified instance must be running or the SUBMIT call will fail.

The INSTANCE procedure alters the instance affinity of an existing entry in the calling user's job queue.

INTERVAL

```
DBMS_JOB.INTERVAL(
    job      IN BINARY_INTEGER,
    interval IN VARCHAR2 DEFAULT 'null' );
```

Table 4-8   DBMS_JOB.INTERVAL Parameters

Parameter	Description
job	Indicates the number of the job to be changed.
Interval	Gives a PL/SQL expression, to be used to calculate subsequent run times.

The INTERVAL procedure alters the run interval calculation expression for an existing entry in the calling user's job queue.

BROKEN

```
DBMS_JOB.BROKEN (
    job      IN BINARY_INTEGER,
    broken   IN BOOLEAN,
    what     IN VARCHAR2 );
```

Table 4-9   DBMS_JOB.BROKEN Parameters

Parameter	Description
job	Indicates the number of the job to be changed.
broken	Indicates if a job is broken or not. A value of TRUE indicates that the job is broken, and thus disabled.
next_date	Indicates the initial run time.

The BROKEN procedure alters the broken status of an existing entry in the calling user's job queue. If this procedure is called while a job is running, the job's status is reset, as normal, when the job exits. Therefore, this procedure should only be called when the job in question is not running.

RUN

```
DBMS_JOB.RUN (
    job     IN BINARY_INTEGER,
    force   IN BOOLEAN DEFAULT FALSE ) ;
```

Table 4-10   DBMS_JOB.RUN Parameters

Parameter	Description
job	Indicates the number of the job to be run.
force	If set to TRUE, instance affinity is ignored for this job run. If set to FALSE, the job can be successfully run only on the instance to which it has been assigned.

The RUN procedure is used to immediately run an existing entry in the calling user's job queue. The job runs in the user's session, in the foreground. When the job exits, its broken flag is set or reset as normal, and the next run date is recalculated.

USER_EXPORT

```
DBMS_JOB.USER_EXPORT (
    job     IN    BINARY_INTEGER,
    mycall  IN OUT VARCHAR2 ) ;


DBMS_JOB.USER_EXPORT (
    job     IN     BINARY_INTEGER,
    mycall  IN OUT VARCHAR2,
    myinst  IN OUT VARCHAR2 ) ;
```

Table 4-11   DBMS_JOB.USER_EXPORT Parameters

Parameter	Description
job	Indicates the number of the job to be exported.
mycall	Used to return the text of a statement, which can be used to recreate the job.
myinst	Used to return the text of a statement to alter the newly recreated job's instance affinity.

The USER_EXPORT procedure allows you to copy an existing job, or save its definition outside the database. The procedure is overloaded, and the three-argument version also allows copying or saving a job's instance affinity, along with the rest of its definition.

DBMS_SCHEDULER

CREATE_JOB

```
DBMS_JOB.CREATE_JOB(
  -- Creates a job with inline program and schedule

  job_name           IN VARCHAR2,
  job_type           IN VARCHAR2,
  job_action         IN VARCHAR2,
  number_of_arguments IN PLS_INTEGER DEFAULT 0,
  start_date         IN TIMESTAMP WITH TIME ZONE DEFAULT NULL,
  repeat_interval    IN VARCHAR2 DEFAULT NULL,
  end_date           IN TIMESTAMP WITH TIME ZONE DEFAULT NULL,
  job_class          IN VARCHAR2 DEFAULT 'DEFAULT_JOB_CLASS',
  enabled            IN BOOLEAN DEFAULT FALSE,
  auto_drop          IN BOOLEAN DEFAULT TRUE,
  comments           IN VARCHAR2 DEFAULT NULL );


DBMS_JOB.CREATE_JOB(
  -- Creates a job with predefined program and schedule

  job_name           IN VARCHAR2,
```

```
program_name    IN VARCHAR2,
schedule_name    IN VARCHAR2,
job_class        IN VARCHAR2 DEFAULT 'DEFAULT_JOB_CLASS',
enabled          IN BOOLEAN DEFAULT FALSE,
auto_drop        IN BOOLEAN DEFAULT TRUE,
comments         IN VARCHAR2 DEFAULT NULL );

DBMS_JOB.CREATE_JOB(
-- Creates a job with predefined program and inline schedule
job_name         IN VARCHAR2,
program_name     IN VARCHAR2,
start_date       IN TIMESTAMP WITH TIME ZONE DEFAULT NULL,
repeat_interval  IN VARCHAR2 DEFAULT NULL,
end_date         IN TIMESTAMP WITH TIME ZONE DEFAULT NULL,
job_class        IN VARCHAR2 DEFAULT 'DEFAULT_JOB_CLASS',
enabled          IN BOOLEAN DEFAULT FALSE,
auto_drop        IN BOOLEAN DEFAULT TRUE,
comments         IN VARCHAR2 DEFAULT NULL );

DBMS_JOB.CREATE_JOB(
-- Creates a job with inline program and predefined schedule
```

```
job_name            IN VARCHAR2,
schedule_name       IN VARCHAR2,
job_type            IN VARCHAR2,
job_action          IN VARCHAR2,
number_of_arguments IN PLS_INTEGER DEFAULT 0,
job_class           IN VARCHAR2 DEFAULT 'DEFAULT_JOB_CLASS',
enabled             IN BOOLEAN DEFAULT FALSE,
auto_drop           IN BOOLEAN DEFAULT TRUE,
comments            IN VARCHAR2 DEFAULT NULL );
```

Table 4-12 DBMS_SCHEDULE.CREATE_JOB Parameters

Parameter	Description
job_name	Specifies the name of the job to be created. This name must be unique in the SQL namespace.
job_type	Indicates the type of job to be created. Valid values are plsql_block, stored_procedure, and executable.

Table 4-12   DBMS_SCHEDULE.CREATE_JOB Parameters (continued)

Parameter	Description
job_action	Defines the job's action. If job_type is set to plsql_block, this string should be an anonymous PL/SQL block. If job_type is set to stored_procedure, this should be the stored procedure's name, qualified as necessary. For a job_type of executable, this string should be the fully qualified name of the program to be run, including any fixed command line arguments.
number_of_arguments	Specifies how many arguments should be supplied for this job. If job_type is plsql_block, this parameter must be zero.
program_name	The name of the predefined program associated with this job, if any.
start_date	For a non-repeating job, this value specifies when the job should be run. For a repeating job, this parameter defines the initial time at which the job will be eligible to run, and the repeat_interval expression is used to determine its actual initial run time. If start_date is set to a time in the past, the current time is used instead. If both start_date and repeat_interval are left null, the job runs as soon as it is submitted.
repeat_interval	This parameter is used to determine when and how often a job should repeat. Both calendaring and PL/SQL expressions are acceptable. If this parameter is not specified, the job will run only once, based on the start_date parameter.

Table 4-12 DBMS_SCHEDULE.CREATE_JOB Parameters *(continued)*

Parameter	Description
schedule_name	Specifies the predefined schedule, window, or window group to be used for this job.
end_date	Supplies a date after which this job will no longer be executed. When the given date is passed, the job's state will be set to COMPLETED and its enabled flag will be set to FALSE.
job_class	Specifies that the job belongs to the provided job class. If no class is specified, the job is assigned to the default class.
enabled	Determines if the job is enabled or disabled when it is created. By default, this flag is set to FALSE and can be changed later with the ENABLE and/or DISABLE procedures.
auto_drop	Determines whether or not the job should be retained in the queue after it has been run once (for non-repeating jobs), or when it is marked as COMPLETED (for repeating jobs). If set to TRUE, the job is removed from the queue when it's finished. If set to FALSE, the job is retained until explicitly dropped.
comments	Optional comment.

The CREATE_JOB procedure creates a new entry in the indicated job queue.

RUN_JOB

```
DBMS_JOB.RUN_JOB (
    job_name    IN VARCHAR2 ) ;
```

Table 4-13 DBMS_SCHEDULE.RUN_JOB Parameters

Parameter	Description
job_name	Specifies the name of the job to be run.

The RUN_JOB procedure immediately executes the designated job in the calling user's current session.

STOP_JOB

```
DBMS_JOB.STOP_JOB (
job_name      IN VARCHAR2,
force         IN BOOLEAN DEFAULT FALSE ) ;
```

Table 4-14 DBMS_SCHEDULE.STOP_JOB Parameters

Parameter	Description
job_name	Specifies the name of the job or job class to be stopped. For a job class, the SYS schema should precede the class name.
force	If job fails to stop gracefully, the job slave process will be terminated, if the force parameter is set to TRUE. If set to FALSE, this procedure will return an error if the indicated job fails to stop gracefully.

The STOP_JOB procedure attempts to stop the indicated job, if it is running.

COPY_JOB

```
DBMS_JOB.COPY_JOB(
    old_job      IN VARCHAR2,
    new_job      IN VARCHAR2 );
```

Table 4-15 DBMS_SCHEDULE.COPY_JOB Parameters

Parameter	Description
old_job	Specifies the name of the existing job, which will be copied.
new_job	Provides the name to which the old job will be copied.

The COPY_JOB procedure is used to copy an existing job to a new job name. All aspects of the job remain unchanged except the name, which is changed to the value of the new_job parameter, and the status, which is set to DISABLED.

DROP_JOB

```
DBMS_JOB.DROP_JOB(
job_name        IN VARCHAR2,
force           IN BOOLEAN DEFAULT FALSE );
```

Table 4-16   DBMS_SCHEDULE.DROP_JOB Parameters

Parameter	Description
job_name	Specifies the name of the job to be dropped.
force	If the job to be dropped is running when DROP_JOB is called, an error will be returned, unless force is set to TRUE. If force is TRUE, the job will be stopped, then dropped.

The DROP_JOB procedure attempts to remove the indicated job from the job queue.

SET_JOB_ARGUMENT_VALUE

```
DBMS_JOB.SET_JOB_ARGUMENT_VALUE (
job_name        IN VARCHAR2,
argument_position  IN PLS_INTEGER,
argument_value   IN VARCHAR2 ) ;

DBMS_JOB.SET_JOB_ARGUMENT_VALUE (
job_name        IN VARCHAR2,
argument_name    IN VARCHAR2,
argument_value   IN VARCHAR2 ) ;
```

Table 4-17 DBMS_SCHEDULE.SET_JOB_ARGUMENT_VALUE Parameters

Parameter	Description
job_name	Specifies the name of the job or job class to be altered. For a job class, the SYS schema should precede the class name.
argument_name	Indicates the name of the argument to be set.
argument_position	Indicates the numeric position of the argument to be set.
argument_value	Provides the new value to which the argument should be set.

The SET_JOB_ARGUMENT_VALUE procedure provides non-default arguments for the program associated with a job or job class. Setting a job argument value overrides any default defined in the program.

SET_JOB_ANYDATA_VALUE

```
DBMS_JOB.SET_JOB_ANYDATA_VALUE (
    job_name          IN VARCHAR2,
    argument_position IN PLS_INTEGER,
    argument_value    IN SYS.ANYDATA ) ;

DBMS_JOB.SET_JOB_ANYDATA_VALUE (
    job_name          IN VARCHAR2,
    argument_name     IN VARCHAR2,
    argument_value    IN SYS.ANYDATA ) ;
```

Table 4-18   DBMS_SCHEDULE.SET_JOB_ANYDATA_VALUE Parameters

Parameter	Description
job_name	Specifies the name of the job or job class to be altered. For a job class, the SYS schema should precede the class name.
argument_name	Indicates the name of the argument to be set.
argument_position	Indicates the numeric position of the argument to be set.
argument_value	Provides the new value to which the argument should be set, encapsulated in an AnyData object.

The SET_JOB_ANYDATA_VALUE procedure provides non-default arguments for the program associated with a job or job class. The AnyData object should be used for parameters that aren't strings and can't be automatically converted to or from strings. Setting a job argument value overrides any default defined in the program.

RESET_JOB_ARGUMENT_VALUE

```
DBMS_JOB.RESET_JOB_ARGUMENT_VALUE (
  job_name           IN VARCHAR2,
  argument_position  IN PLS_INTEGER ) ;

DBMS_JOB.RESET_JOB_ARGUMENT_VALUE (
  job_name       IN VARCHAR2,
  argument_name  IN VARCHAR2 ) ;
```

Table 4-19 DBMS_SCHEDULE. RESET_JOB_ARGUMENT_VALUE Parameters

Parameter	Description
job_name	Specifies the name of the job or job class to be altered. For a job class, the SYS schema should precede the class name.
argument_name	Indicates the name of the argument to be set.
argument_position	Indicates the numeric position of the argument to be set.

The RESET_JOB_ARGUMENT_VALUE procedure sets the defined argument to NULL, or back to the defined default, if any. If no default is defined, the job is disabled.

CREATE_JOB_CLASS

```
DBMS_JOB.CREATE_JOB_CLASS (
job_class_name          IN VARCHAR2,
resource_consumer_group IN VARCHAR2 DEFAULT NULL,
service                 IN VARCHAR2 DEFAULT NULL,
logging_level           IN PLS_INTEGER DEFAULT NULL,
log_history             IN PLS_INTEGER DEFAULT NULL,
comments                IN VARCHAR2 DEFAULT NULL );
```

Table 4-20   DBMS_SCHEDULE. CREATE_JOB_CLASS Parameters

Parameter	Description
job_class_name	Specifies the name of the job class to be created. A schema other than SYS may not be specified.
resource_consumer_group	Specifies the resource consumer group with which this job class should be associated. If the associated resource consumer group is dropped, or if no resource consumer group is indicated, the job class will be assigned to the default resource consumer group.

Table 4-20 DBMS_SCHEDULE. CREATE_JOB_CLASS Parameters *(continued)*

Parameter	Description
service	Indicates the service to which the job class belongs. Belonging to a given service will cause jobs in that class to only run in instances that have the given service assigned. If no services are assigned, there will be no service affinity.
logging_level	Specifies how much information to log. Allowed values are **DBMS_SCHEDULER.LOGGING_OFF**, **DBMS_SCHEDULER_LOGGING_RUNS**, and **DBMS_SCHEDULER.LOGGING_FULL**.
log_history	Indicates how many days of history should be retained in the logs. The default is 30 days.
comments	Optional comment.

The CREATE_JOB_CLASS procedure adds a new job class object. Job classes are always created in the SYS schema.

DROP_JOB_CLASS

```
DBMS_JOB.DROP_JOB_CLASS (
job_class_name    IN VARCHAR2,
force             IN BOOLEAN DEFAULT FALSE ) ;
```

Table 4-21   DBMS_SCHEDULE. DROP_JOB_CLASS Parameters

Parameter	Description
job_class_name	Specifies the name of the job class to be dropped. A schema other than SYS may not be specified.
force	If force is set to FALSE and there are jobs assigned to this job class, the procedure returns an error. If set to TRUE, jobs belonging to the class are disabled, and the job class is dropped.

The DROP_JOB_CLASS procedure adds a new job class object. Job classes are always created in the SYS schema.

CREATE_PROGRAM

```
DBMS_JOB.CREATE_PROGRAM (
program_name        IN VARCHAR2,
program_type        IN VARCHAR2,
program_action      IN VARCHAR2,
number_of_arguments IN PLS_INTEGER DEFAULT 0,
enabled             IN BOOLEAN DEFAULT FALSE,
comments            IN VARCHAR2 DEFAULT NULL );
```

Table 4-22 DBMS_SCHEDULE.CREATE_PROGRAM Parameters

Parameter	Description
program_name	Specifies the name of the program to be created. This name must be unique in the SQL namespace.
program_type	Indicates the type of program to be created. Valid values are plsql_block, stored_procedure, and executable.

Table 4-22 DBMS_SCHEDULE.CREATE_PROGRAM Parameters *(continued)*

Parameter	Description
program_action	Defines the program's action. If program_type is set to plsql_block, this string should be an anonymous PL/SQL block. If program_type is stored_procedure, this should be the stored procedure's name, qualified as necessary. For a program_type of executable, this string should be the fully qualified name of the program to be run, including any fixed command line arguments.
number_of_arguments	Specifies how many arguments should be supplied for this program. If program_type is plsql_block, this parameter must be zero.
enabled	The enabled flag determines if the program is enabled or disabled when it is created. By default, this flag is set to FALSE, and can be changed later with the ENABLE and/or DISABLE procedures.
comments	Optional comment.

The CREATE_PROGRAM procedure creates a new predefined program object.

DROP_PROGRAM

```
DBMS_JOB.DROP_PROGRAM (
program_name    IN VARCHAR2,
force           IN BOOLEAN DEFAULT FALSE ) ;
```

Table 4-23 DBMS_SCHEDULE.DROP_PROGRAM Parameters

Parameter	Description
program_name	Specifies the name of the program to be dropped. This name must be unique in the SQL namespace.
force	If force is set to FALSE and there are jobs referencing the program, the procedure will fail. If set to TRUE, associated jobs will be disabled, and then the program will be dropped.

The DROP_PROGRAM procedure removes a predefined program object.

DEFINE_PROGRAM_ARGUMENT

```
DBMS_JOB.DEFINE_PROGRAM_ARGUMENT (
program_name            IN VARCHAR2,
argument_name           IN VARCHAR2 DEFAULT NULL,
argument_position       IN PLS_INTEGER,
argument_type           IN VARCHAR2 DEFAULT NULL,
argument_default_value  IN VARCHAR2 DEFAULT NULL,
out_argument            IN BOOLEAN DEFAULT FALSE ) ;
```

Table 4-24   DBMS_SCHEDULE.DEFINE_PROGRAM_ARGUMENT Parameters

Parameter	Description
program_name	Specifies the name of the program to be altered.
argument_name	Indicates the name of the argument to be set. If a name is specified, it must be unique.
argument_position	Indicates the numeric position of the argument to be set. The first argument is number 1, not zero.

Table 4-24 DBMS_SCHEDULE.DEFINE_PROGRAM_ARGUMENT Parameters

argument_type	This is a purely informational field, intended to indicate the type of argument that should be supplied. It is not used or validated by the scheduler in any way.
argument_value	Provides the default value to which the argument should be set. When associated with a job, the value may be overridden in the job definition.
out_argument	This parameter should always be set to FALSE in the current release.

The DEFINE_PROGRAM_ARGUMENT procedure provides default values for arguments used by the indicated program.

DEFINE_ANYDATA_ARGUMENT

```
DBMS_JOB.DEFINE_ANYDATA_ARGUMENT (
    program_name            IN VARCHAR2,
    argument_name           IN VARCHAR2 DEFAULT NULL,
    argument_position       IN PLS_INTEGER,
    argument_type           IN VARCHAR2 DEFAULT NULL,
    argument_default_value  IN SYS.ANYDATA DEFAULT NULL,
    out_argument            IN BOOLEAN DEFAULT FALSE ) ;
```

Table 4-25   DBMS_SCHEDULE.DEFINE_ANYDATA_ARGUMENT Parameters

Parameter	Description
program_name	Specifies the name of the program to be altered.
argument_name	Indicates the name of the argument to be set. If a name is specified, it must be unique.
argument_position	Indicates the numeric position of the argument to be set. The first argument is number 1, not zero.
argument_type	This is a purely informational field, intended to indicate the type of argument that should be supplied. It is not used or validated by the scheduler in any way.

Table 4-25 DBMS_SCHEDULE.DEFINE_ANYDATA_ARGUMENT Parameters (continued)

Parameter	Description
argument_value	Provides the default value to which the argument should be set, encapsulated in an AnyData object. When associated with a job, the value may be overridden in the job definition.
out_argument	This parameter should always be set to FALSE in the current release.

The DEFINE_ANYDATA_ARGUMENT procedure provides default values for arguments used by the indicated program. The AnyData object should be used for parameters that aren't strings, and can't be automatically converted to or from strings.

DEFINE_METADATA_ARGUMENT

```
DBMS_JOB.DEFINE_METADATA_ARGUMENT (
    program_name        IN VARCHAR2,
    metadata_attribute  IN VARCHAR2,
    argument_position   IN PLS_INTEGER,
    argument_name       IN VARCHAR2 DEFAULT NULL );
```

Table 4-26   DBMS_SCHEDULE.DEFINE_METADATA_ARGUMENT Parameters

Parameter	Description
program_name	Specifies the name of the program to be altered.
metadata_attribute	Defines which metadata attribute should be passed as the indicated argument. Valid values are job_name, job_owner, job_start, window_start, and window_end.
argument_position	Indicates the numeric position of the argument to be set. The first argument is number 1, not zero.
argument_name	Indicates the name of the argument to be set. If a name is specified, it must be unique.

The DEFINE_METADATA_ARGUMENT procedure provides metadata values for arguments used by the indicated program. Metadata values provide a program with information about the job environment in which it is executing. These arguments may not be overridden by jobs associated with the program.

DROP_PROGRAM_ARGUMENT

```
DBMS_JOB.DROP_PROGRAM_ARGUMENT (
program_name      IN VARCHAR2,
argument_position   IN PLS_INTEGER  ) ;

DBMS_JOB.DROP_PROGRAM_ARGUMENT (
program_name      IN VARCHAR2,
argument_name     IN VARCHAR2 DEFAULT NULL ) ;
```

Table 4-27 DBMS_SCHEDULE.DROP_PROGRAM_ARGUMENT Parameters

Parameter	Description
program_name	Specifies the name of the program to be altered.
argument_name	Indicates the name of the argument to be dropped.
argument_position	Indicates the numeric position of the argument to be dropped.

The DROP_PROGRAM_ARGUMENT procedure removes default values for arguments used by the indicated program.

CREATE_SCHEDULE

```
DBMS_JOB.CREATE_SCHEDULE (
   schedule_name   IN VARCHAR2,
   start_date      IN TIMESTAMP WITH TIME ZONE DEFAULT NULL,
   repeat_interval IN VARCHAR2,
   end_date        IN TIMESTAMP WITH TIME ZONE DEFAULT NULL,
   comments        IN VARCHAR2 DEFAULT NULL ) ;
```

Table 4-28 DBMS_SCHEDULE.CREATE_SCHEDULE Parameters

Parameter	Description
schedule_name	Specifies the name of the schedule to be created.
start_date	Specifies the time at which this schedule becomes valid. For a repeating schedule, this is a reference value, and the repeat_interval value is used to determine the first schedule instance that falls after start_date. If the specified start_date is in the past and no repeat_interval is supplied, the procedure will fail.

Table 4-28 DBMS_SCHEDULE.CREATE_SCHEDULE Parameters *(continued)*

Parameter	Description
repeat_interval	This parameter is used to determine when and how often a schedule should repeat. Only calendaring expressions are acceptable. If this parameter is not specified, the schedule will run only once, based on the start_date parameter.
end_date	Indicates the time after which jobs will not run and windows will not open. A non-repeating schedule that has no end date will be valid forever.
comments	Optional comment.

The CREATE_SCHEDULE procedure creates a new predefined schedule object.

DROP_SCHEDULE

```
DBMS_JOB.DROP_SCHEDULE (
  schedule_name  IN VARCHAR2,
  force          IN BOOLEAN DEFAULT FALSE ) ;
```

Table 4-29 *DBMS_SCHEDULE.DROP_SCHEDULE Parameters*

Parameter	Description
schedule_name	Specifies the name of the schedule to be dropped.
force	If force is set to FALSE, and there are jobs or windows referencing the schedule, the procedure will fail. If set to TRUE, associated jobs or windows will be disabled, and then the schedule will be dropped.

The DROP_SCHEDULE procedure removes an existing predefined schedule object.

CREATE_WINDOW

```
DBMS_JOB.CREATE_WINDOW(
window_name     IN VARCHAR2,
resource_plan   IN VARCHAR2,
schedule_name   IN VARCHAR2,
duration        IN INTERVAL DAY TO SECOND,
window_priority IN VARCHAR2 DEFAULT 'LOW',
comments        IN VARCHAR2 DEFAULT NULL );

DBMS_JOB.CREATE_WINDOW(
window_name     IN VARCHAR2,
resource_plan   IN VARCHAR2,
start_date      IN TIMESTAMP WITH TIME ZONE DEFAULT NULL,
repeat_interval IN VARCHAR2,
end_date        IN TIMESTAMP WITH TIME ZONE DEFAULT NULL,
duration        IN INTERVAL DAY TO SECOND,
window_priority IN VARCHAR2 DEFAULT 'LOW',
comments        IN VARCHAR2 DEFAULT NULL );
```

Table 4-30 DBMS_SCHEDULE.CREATE_WINDOW Parameters

Parameter	Description
window_name	Specifies the name of the window to be created.
resource_plan	Defines the resource plan to be associated with this window. When the window opens, the system will switch to using this resource plan. When the window closes, the original resource plan will be restored.
start_date	For a non-repeating window, specifies the first time at which the window is scheduled to open. If the time is in the past or is not specified, the window will open as soon as it is created. If the window is created with a repeat_interval, this is a reference date, and the actual initial opening time will be determined by the first interval that falls after start_date.
repeat_interval	This parameter is used to determine when and how often a window should repeat. Only calendaring expressions are acceptable. If this parameter is not specified, the window will open only once, based on the start_date parameter.
end_date	Indicates the time after which the window will not open. When the time specified by end_date is passed, the window will be disabled. If no end_date is specified, a repeating window will continue to repeat forever.
schedule_name	Specifies the predefined schedule, window, or window group to be used for this job.

Table 4-30 DBMS_SCHEDULE.CREATE_WINDOW Parameters (continued)

Parameter	Description
duration	Specifies how long the window will remain open.
window_priority	Specifies the window's priority. The only valid values are LOW and HIGH. Windows should not be scheduled to overlap, but if they are, this priority is used to determine which window should take precedence. LOW is the default priority.
comments	Optional comment.

The CREATE_WINDOW procedure creates a new window object. Windows are always created in the SYS schema.

DROP_WINDOW

```
DBMS_JOB.DROP_WINDOW(
window_name  IN VARCHAR2,
force        IN BOOLEAN DEFAULT FALSE );
```

Table 4-31 DBMS_SCHEDULE.DROP_WINDOW Parameters

Parameter	Description
window_name	Specifies the name of the window to be dropped.
force	If force is set to FALSE, and the window to be dropped is currently open, the procedure will fail. If set to TRUE, the window will be closed, then dropped.

The DROP_WINDOW procedure removes an existing window object. All jobs that use the window as a schedule will be disabled, though currently running jobs will not be stopped. Dropping a window will automatically remove it from any window groups of which it was a member.

OPEN_WINDOW

```
DBMS_JOB.OPEN_WINDOW (
window_name   IN VARCHAR2,
duration      IN INTERVAL DAY TO SECOND,
force         IN BOOLEAN DEFAULT FALSE ) ;
```

Table 4-32 DBMS_SCHEDULE.OPEN_WINDOW Parameters

Parameter	Description
window_name	Specifies the name of the window to be opened.
duration	Specifies how long the window will remain open.
force	If force is set to FALSE, and another window is already open, the procedure will fail. If set to TRUE, the other window will be closed, then the new window will open.

The OPEN_WINDOW procedure opens an existing window object prematurely. The next open time for the window will not change.

CLOSE_WINDOW

```
DBMS_JOB.CLOSE_WINDOW(
window_name    IN VARCHAR2  );
```

Table 4-33   *DBMS_SCHEDULE.CLOSE_WINDOW Parameters*

Parameter	Description
window_name	Specifies the name of the window to be closed.

The CLOSE_WINDOW procedure closes an open window prematurely.

CREATE_WINDOW_GROUP

```
DBMS_JOB.CREATE_WINDOW_GROUP (
   group_name   IN VARCHAR2,
   window_list  IN VARCHAR2 DEFAULT NULL,
   comments     IN VARCHAR2 DEFAULT NULL );
```

Table 4-34 DBMS_SCHEDULE.CREATE_WINDOW_GROUP Parameters

Parameter	Description
group_name	Specifies the name of the window group to be created.
window_list	A list of one or more windows to be assigned to the window group.
comments	Optional comment.

The CREATE_WINDOW_GROUP procedure creates a new window group object. Window groups always reside in the SYS schema. Window groups can't contain other window groups.

ADD_WINDOW_GROUP_MEMBER

```
DBMS_JOB.ADD_WINDOW_GROUP_MEMBER (
  group_name    IN VARCHAR2,
  window_list IN VARCHAR2 DEFAULT NULL ) ;
```

Table 4-35   DBMS_SCHEDULE.ADD_WINDOW_GROUP_MEMBER Parameters

Parameter	Description
group_name	Specifies the name of the window group to be altered.
window_list	A list of one or more windows to be assigned to the window group.

The ADD_WINDOW_GROUP_MEMBER procedure adds one or more windows to an existing window group.

REMOVE_WINDOW_GROUP_MEMBER

```
DBMS_JOB.REMOVE_WINDOW_GROUP_MEMBER (
  group_name   IN VARCHAR2,
  window_list  IN VARCHAR2 DEFAULT NULL );
```

Table 4-36 DBMS_SCHEDULE.REMOVE_WINDOW_GROUP_MEMBER Parameters

Parameter	Description
group_name	Specifies the name of the window group to be altered.
window_list	A list of one or more windows to be dropped from the window group.

The REMOVE_WINDOW_GROUP_MEMBER procedure drops one or more windows from an existing window group.

DROP_WINDOW_GROUP

```
DBMS_JOB.DROP_WINDOW_GROUP (
group_name    IN VARCHAR2,
force         IN BOOLEAN DEFAULT FALSE );
```

Table 4-37   DBMS_SCHEDULE.DROP_WINDOW_GROUP Parameters

Parameter	Description
group_name	Specifies the name of the window group to be dropped.
force	If force is set to FALSE and the window group to be dropped is being used as the schedule for any job, the procedure will fail. If set to TRUE, the job(s) will be disabled, then the window group will be dropped. Any jobs currently running will be allowed to finish, unless the job specifies that it is to be stopped on window close.

The DROP_WINDOW_GROUP procedure removes an existing window group. All jobs that use the window as a schedule will be disabled, though currently running jobs will not be stopped.

ENABLE

```
DBMS_JOB.ENABLE (
   name   IN VARCHAR2 ) ;
```

Table 4-38 DBMS_SCHEDULE.ENABLE Parameters

Parameter	Description
name	Specifies the name of the item to be enabled.

The ENABLE procedure is used to enable a program, job, window, or window group. Validity checks are performed before enabling an object. Because the ENABLE procedure is not specific to windows, window names must be preceded by "SYS".

DISABLE

```
DBMS_JOB.DISABLE(
name  IN VARCHAR2,
force IN BOOLEAN DEFAULT FALSE );
```

Table 4-39   DBMS_SCHEDULE.DISABLE Parameters

Parameter	Description
name	Specifies the name of the item to be disabled.
force	If force is set to FALSE, the procedure will fail if the name is set to a program and there are jobs pointing to the program, or if the name is set to a window or window group and a job has the window or window group as its schedule. If force is set to TRUE, the DISABLE will succeed, but no dependent objects will be altered.

The DISABLE procedure is used to disable a program, job, window, or window group. Because the DISABLE procedure is not specific to windows, window names must be preceded by "SYS".

SET_ATTRIBUTE

```
DBMS_JOB.SET_ATTRIBUTE (
name    IN VARCHAR2,
attribute IN VARCHAR2,
value   IN [ VARCHAR2, TIMESTAMP WITH TIME ZONE, PLS_INTEGER, BOOLEAN, INTERVAL
DAY TO SECOND ] );
```

Table 4-40 DBMS_SCHEDULE.SET_ATTRIBUTE Parameters

Parameter	Description
name	Specifies the name of the item to be altered.
attribute	See Tables 4-41 to 4-53 to find which attributes are valid for which items.
value	The new value being set for the attribute.

The SET_ATTRIBUTE procedure is used to alter existing scheduler objects. This is an overloaded procedure, supporting value arguments of five different types, as shown in the syntax example above. If the object is enabled, it will be disabled, the attribute will be altered, and it will be re-enabled afterward. If the object can't be re-enabled, an error will be generated, and the object will be left disabled.

The attributes that can be modified for programs are described in Table 4-41:

Table 4-41   DBMS_SCHEDULER.SET_ATTRIBUTE Parameters for Programs

Name	Description
program_action	Specifies the action to be performed.
program_type	Specifies the type of program. Possible values are plsql_block, stored_procedure, and executable.
number_of_arguments	Identifies how many arguments are to be passed to the program.
comments	Optional description of the program.

The attributes that can be modified for schedules are described in Table 4-42:

Table 4-42   DBMS_SCHEDULE.SET_ATTRIBUTE Parameters for Schedules

Name	Description
repeat_interval	An interval expression that uses the calendar syntax.
comments	Optional comment.
end_date	The cutoff date after which the schedule is invalid.
start_date	Start or reference date used by the repeat_interval setting.

The attributes that can be modified for jobs are described in Table 4-43:

Table 4-43   *DBMS_SCHEDULE.SET_ATTRIBUTE Parameters for Jobs*

Name	Description
logging_level	Designates how much information is logged. Possible values are DBMS_SCHEDULER.LOGGING_OFF, DBMS_SCHEDULER.LOGGING_RUNS, and DBMS_SCHEDULER.LOGGING_FULL.
restartable	Specifies whether a job can be restarted after a failure. Jobs can be restarted by default, meaning that a job will immediately be restarted from the beginning if it fails. The job will be retried up to five times, before the error count is incremented.
max_failures	Defines the number of times a job can fail before it's disabled by the scheduler and marked as broken.
max_runs	Tells the scheduler to disable a job after a number of successful runs equal to this value.
job_weight	Sets the default parallelism for SQL used inside the job. The range is 1–100.

Table 4-43 DBMS_SCHEDULE.SET_ATTRIBUTE Parameters for Jobs *(continued)*

Name	Description
instance_stickiness	This attribute defaults to TRUE. When set to TRUE in a RAC environment, the job will initially run on the least loaded instance. After the initial run, the job will always try to run on the same instance it used before. If the instance to which the job is "stuck" is down or overloaded and unable to run the job, it will go ahead and run on another instance. If this attribute is set to FALSE, the job will always run on the available instance with the lightest load. In a non-RAC environment, this attribute is essentially meaningless.
stop_on_window_exit	This attribute defaults to FALSE. If set to TRUE and the job's schedule is a window or window group, the job will be stopped using the STOP_JOB procedure when the window closes.
job_priority	Specifies the priority of this job relative to others in the same job class. If multiple jobs in the same class are scheduled to be run at the same time, the highest priority job is run first. The range is 1 to 5, with 1 being the highest priority.
schedule_limit	In resource-constrained systems, jobs may not always be started on time. This attribute specifies that a job run should be skipped completely, rather than started later than its normal time plus the interval specified in the schedule_limit. Skipped runs are logged as skipped and don't count as either successful or failed runs.

Table 4-43 DBMS_SCHEDULE.SET_ATTRIBUTE Parameters for Jobs (continued)

Name	Description
program_name	Indicates the name of a predefined program to use with this job.
job_action	Defines the task for this job to run.
job_type	Defines the type of task for this job to run. Valid values are plsql_block, stored_procedure, and executable.
number_of_arguments	Indicates the number of arguments for the specified job_action. If the program_name attribute is set, this attribute should be NULL.
schedule_name	Indicates the name of a predefined schedule to use with this job.
repeat_interval	Either a PL/SQL expression returning the next date on which to run or a calendar syntax expression. If schedule_name is set, this attribute should be NULL.
start_date	Defines the original date on which this job started or is scheduled to start. If schedule_name is set, this attribute should be NULL.
end_date	Indicates a date after which the job will no longer run. If schedule_name is set, this attribute should be NULL.
job_class	Specifies the class with which this job is associated.

Table 4-43 DBMS_SCHEDULE.SET_ATTRIBUTE Parameters for Jobs (continued)

Name	Description
comments	Optional comment.
auto_drop	If set to TRUE, the job will be dropped when it is complete.

The attributes that can be modified for job classes are described in Table 4-44:

Table 4-44 DBMS_SCHEDULE.SET_ATTRIBUTE Parameters for Job Classes

Name	Description
resource_consumer_group	Sets the resource_consumer_group to which this job class belongs.
service	Defines the service database object to which this job class belongs. Note that this is not a tnsnames.ora service name.
log_purge_policy	Instructs the scheduler if and when to purge log table entries for jobs belonging to this class.
comments	Optional comment.

The attributes that can be modified for windows are described in Table 4-45:

Table 4-45   DBMS_SCHEDULE.SET_ATTRIBUTE Parameters for Windows

Name	Description
resource_plan	Defines the resource plan that is to be associated with this window. When the window opens, the system will switch to using this resource plan. When the window closes, the original resource plan will be restored.
window_priority	Defines the window priority. The only allowed values are LOW and HIGH. LOW is the default.
duration	Sets the duration for which the window is open, in minutes.
schedule_name	Names a predefined schedule that is to be used with this window.
repeat_interval	An interval string that uses the calendar syntax. PL/SQL date expressions are not allowed for windows. If this is set, schedule_name must be NULL.
start_date	The next date on which the window is scheduled to open. If this is set, schedule_name must be NULL.

Table 4-45 DBMS_SCHEDULE.SET_ATTRIBUTE Parameters for Windows (continued)

Name	Description
end_date	The date after which the window will no longer open. If this is set, schedule_name must be NULL.
comments	Optional comment.

The attributes which can be modified for window groups are described in Table 4-46:

Table 4-46 DBMS_SCHEDULE.SET_ATTRIBUTE Parameters for Window Groups

Name	Description
comments	Optional comment.

SET_ATTRIBUTE_NULL

```
DBMS_JOB.SET_ATTRIBUTE_NULL (
name   IN VARCHAR2,
attribute IN VARCHAR2 ) ;
```

Table 4-47   DBMS_SCHEDULE.SET_ATTRIBUTE_NULL Parameters

Parameter	Description
name	Specifies the name of the item to be altered.
attribute	See Tables 4-41-4-46, to find which attributes are valid for which items.

The SET_ATTRIBUTE_NULL procedure is used to alter existing scheduler object attributes to NULL. If an object is enabled, it will be disabled, the attribute will be nulled, and it will be re-enabled afterward. If the object can't be re-enabled, an error will be generated, and the object will be left disabled.

GET_ATTRIBUTE

```
DBMS_JOB.GET_ATTRIBUTE (
name     IN VARCHAR2,
attribute IN VARCHAR2,
value    OUT [ VARCHAR2, TIMESTAMP WITH TIME ZONE, PLS_INTEGER, BOOLEAN, INTERVAL
DAY TO SECOND ] );
```

Table 4-48 DBMS_SCHEDULE.GET_ATTRIBUTE Parameters

Parameter	Description
name	Specifies the name of the item to be altered.
attribute	See Tables 4-41-4-46, to find which attributes are valid for which items.
value	The existing value of the attribute.

The GET_ATTRIBUTE procedure is used to retrieve the value of an attribute of an existing scheduler object. This is an overloaded procedure, supporting value arguments of five different types, as shown in the syntax example above.

SET_SCHEDULER_ATTRIBUTE

```
DBMS_JOB.SET_SCHEDULER_ATTRIBUTE (
attribute IN VARCHAR2,
value    IN VARCHAR2 ) ;
```

Table 4-49   DBMS_SCHEDULE.SET_SCHEDULER_ATTRIBUTE Parameters

Parameter	Description
attribute	Sets the name of the scheduler attribute being altered. See Table 4-50 for valid attributes.
value	Defines the new value of the attribute.

The SET_SCHEDULER_ATTRIBUTE procedure is used to change the value of an attribute of the scheduler itself.

The attributes that can be modified for the scheduler are described in Table 4-50

Table 4-50 DBMS_SCHEDULE.SET_SCHEDULER_ATTRIBUTE Parameters

Name	Description
log_history	Defines the default amount of logging the scheduler will perform.
max_job_slave_processes	Sets the maximum number of slave processes for a particular system. The scheduler will never start more than the specified number of processes, though it may start less, depending on need. The default value is NULL, and the range is 1–999.

GET_SCHEDULER_ATTRIBUTE

```
DBMS_JOB.GET_SCHEDULER_ATTRIBUTE (
attribute IN VARCHAR2,
value    OUT VARCHAR2 ) ;
```

Table 4-51   DBMS_SCHEDULE.GET_SCHEDULER_ATTRIBUTE Parameters

Parameter	Description
attribute	Sets the name of the scheduler attribute being altered. See Table 4-52 for valid attributes.
value	Returns the existing value of the attribute.

The GET_SCHEDULER_ATTRIBUTE procedure is used to retrieve the value of an attribute of the scheduler itself.

GENERATE_JOB_NAME

```
DBMS_JOB.GENERATE_JOB_NAME (
    prefix IN VARCHAR2 DEFAULT NULL ) RETURN VARCHAR2 ;
```

Table 4-52   DBMS_SCHEDULE.GENERATE_JOB_NAME Parameter

Parameter	Description
prefix	Defines a string to which the generated unique job name should be appended.

The GENERATE_JOB_NAME function is used to generate a guaranteed unique job name. If a prefix is supplied, the generated name will be appended to it and returned.

PURGE_LOG

```
DBMS_JOB.PURGE_LOG (
log_history IN PLS_INTEGER DEFAULT 0,
which_log   IN VARCHAR2 DEFAULT 'JOB_AND_WINDOW_LOG',
job_name    IN VARCHAR2 DEFAULT NULL );
```

Table 4-53   DBMS_SCHEDULE.PURGE_LOG Parameters

Parameter	Description
log_history	Specifies, in days, how much log history to keep. Valid values are between 0 and 999. A setting of 0 means that no history is retained.
which_log	Indicates the type of log to purge. Valid values are job_log, window_log, job_and_window_log.
job_name	Defines which job-specific entries to purge from the job log. This can be a comma-delimited list of job names and/or job classes. When job_name has a non-NULL value, the value of which_log is ignored.

The PURGE_LOG procedure is used to manually purge data from the job and/or window logs. It need not be used in normal operations since the scheduler automatically purges information once per day based on its attribute settings.

Calendaring Syntax for Repeat_Interval

The calendaring syntax is as follows:

```
repeat_interval = frequency_clause
[";" interval_clause] [";" bymonth_clause] [";" byweekno_clause]
[";" byyearday_clause] [";" bymonthday_clause] [";" byday_clause]
[";" byhour_clause] [";" byminute_clause] [";" bysecond_clause]

frequency_clause = "FREQ" "=" frequency
frequency = "YEARLY" | "MONTHLY" | "WEEKLY" | "DAILY" |
"HOURLY" | "MINUTELY" | "SECONDLY"
interval_clause = "INTERVAL" "=" intervalnum
intervalnum = 1 through 99
bymonth_clause = "BYMONTH" "=" monthlist
monthlist = monthday ( "," monthday) *
month = numeric_month | char_month
numeric_month = 1 | 2 | 3 ... 12
char_month = "JAN" | "FEB" | "MAR" | "APR" | "MAY" | "JUN" |
"JUL" | "AUG" | "SEP" | "OCT" | "NOV" | "DEC"
byweekno_clause = "BYWEEKNO" "=" weeknumber_list
weeknumber_list = weekday ( "," weeknumber) *
```

```
week = [minus] weekno

minus = "-"

weekno = 1 through 53

byyearday_clause = "BYYEARDAY" "=" yearday_list

yearday_list = yearday ( "," yearday)*

yearday = [minus] yeardaynum

yeardaynum = 1 through 366

bymonthday_clause = "BYMONTHDAY" "=" monthday_list

monthday_list = monthday ( "," monthday) *

monthday = [minus] monthdaynum

monthdaynum = 1 through 31

byday_clause = "BYDAY" "=" byday_list

byday_list = byday ( "," byday)*

byday = [weekdaynum] day

weekdaynum = [minus] daynum

daynum = 1 through 53 /* if frequency is yearly */

daynum = 1 through 5 /* if frequency is monthly */

day = "MON" | "TUE" | "WED" | "THU" | "FRI" | "SAT" | "SUN"

byhour_clause = "BYHOUR" "=" hour_list

hour_list = hour ( "," hour)*

hour = 0 through 23
```

```
byminute_clause = "BYMINUTE" "=" minute_list
minute_list = minute ( "," minute)*
minute = 0 through 59
bysecond_clause = "BYSECOND" "=" second_list
second_list = second ( "," second)*
second = 0 through 59
```

In calendaring syntax, an asterisk (*) means 0 or more.

Table 4-54 Calendar Syntax Parameters

Name	Description
freq	Specifies the type of recurrence, and is required. Possible values are YEARLY, MONTHLY, WEEKLY, DAILY, HOURLY, MINUTELY, and SECONDLY.
interval	Defines how often the recurrence repeats. The default is 1, and the maximum is 99.
bymonth	Specifies the month(s) in which the job is to be executed. Month numbers (1–12) and three-letter abbreviations (JAN–DEC) are acceptable.

Table 4-54 Calendar Syntax Parameters (continued)

Name	Description
byweekno	Indicates the numeric week of the year. Valid values are between 1 and 53. The week number follows the ISO-8601 standard. Parts of week 1 may be in the previous year, and parts of week 52 may be in the following year. If there is a week 53, part of it will definitely be in the following year. Byweekno is only valid for YEARLY.
byyearday	Specifies the day of the year, as a number. Valid values are between 1 and 366 and may be negated to count from the end of the year rather than from the beginning.
bymonthday	Indicates the day of the month, as a number. Valid values are between 1 and 31 and may be negated to count from the end of the month rather than from the beginning.
byday	Specifies the day of the week as a three-letter abbreviation (MON–SUN), optionally modified by a positive or negative number. The valid numbers are 1–53 for YEARLY frequencies, and 1–5 for MONTHLY. Negative numbers count from the end of the year or month rather than from the beginning.
byhour	Provides a numeric value between 0 and 23, indicating the hour of the day.
byminute	Provides a numeric value between 0 and 59, indicating the minute of the hour.
bysecond	Provides a numeric value between 0 and 59, indicating the second of the minute.

- The calendar string must start with the *frequency* clause. All other clauses are optional and can be put in any order.

- All clauses are separated by a semicolon and each clause can be present at most once.

- Spaces are allowed between syntax elements and the strings are case insensitive.

- The list of values for a specific BY clause do not need to be ordered.

- When not enough BY clauses are present to determine what the next date is, this information is retrieved from the start date.

- The byweekno clause is only allowed if the frequency is YEARLY. It cannot be used with other frequencies. When it is present, it will return all days in that week number. If you want to limit it to specific days within the week, you have to add a byday clause.

- Note that when the byweekno clause is used, it is possible that the dates returned are from a year other than the current year.

- For those BY clauses that do not have a consistent range of values, you can count backwards by putting a hyphen (-) in front of the numeric value. This is not supported for BY clauses that are fixed in size. In other words, bymonth, byhour, byminute, and bysecond are not supported.

- The basic values for the byday clause are the days of the week. When the frequency is YEARLY or MONTHLY, you are allowed to specify a positive or negative number in front of each day of the week. In the case of YEARLY, BYDAY=40WED indicates the 40th Monday of the year. In the case of MONTHLY, BYDAY=-2SAT indicates the second to last Saturday of the month.

- Note that positive or negative numbers in front of weekdays are not supported for other frequencies, and in the case of YEARLY, the number ranges from –53 ... –1, 1 ... 53, whereas for MONTHLY, it is limited to –5 ... –1, 1...5.

- If no number is present in front of the weekday, it specifies every occurrence of that weekday in the specified frequency.

- The first day of the week is Monday.

INDEX

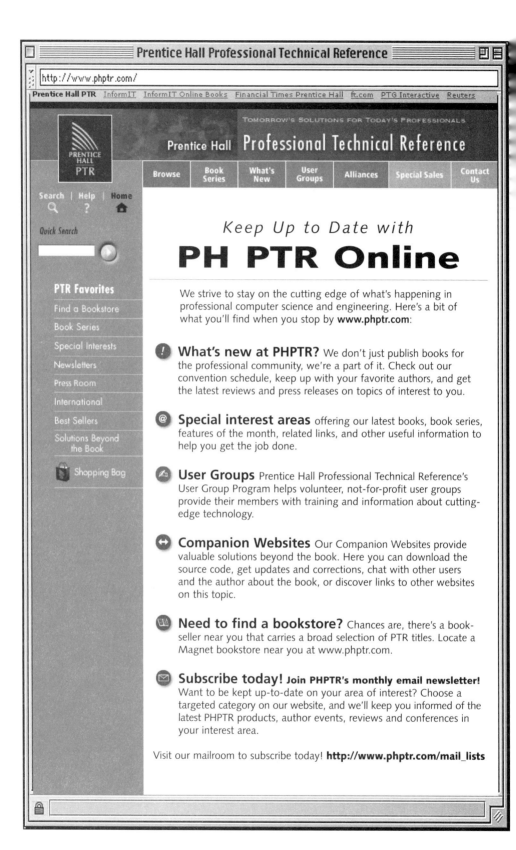